Prime Ministers

Life among the politicians

Wallace Brown

LONGUEVILLE
BOOKS

Longueville Books
PO Box 102
Double Bay, New South Wales, 2028
Australia
www.longuevillebooks.com.au

First published by Longueville Media Pty. Limited

Cartoons by Geoff Pryor
Cover and interior design by Shane Grantham
Typeset in Veljovic by David Longfield
Printed and bound in Australia by McPherson's Printing Group

National Library of Australia
Cataloguing-in-Publication data

Brown, Wallace, 1930–
Ten prime ministers: life among the politicians.
ISBN 1 920681 04 3.
1. Prime ministers—Australia—Biography.
2. Australia—Politics and government—1990–2001.
3. Australia—Politics and government—2001– .
I. Pryor, Geoff, 1944– .
II. Title.

994.04

To
Valerie A Brown,
who urged me, often, to get on with it.

ACKNOWLEDGMENTS

My thanks go to many people whose knowledge and willingness to impart it helped immensely. These include the staff of the Federal Parliamentary Library; former News Ltd Canberra librarian Royce Miosge, who dragged up yellowing newspaper files of yesteryear; Sir Robert Menzies' daughter Heather Henderson, with whom I discussed background aspects of her father's career; Emeritus Professor RG Neale, for information on his research into Australia's involvement in the Vietnam War; former ALP State Secretary Peter Beattie, now Premier of Queensland; and federal MPs and former MPs who sharpened my memory.

My deep appreciation also to Bina Brown of Media Matters for acting as my agent; to publishers David Longfield and Clare Calvet of Longueville Books, whose apt-stated business is to produce *the odd book*; to efficient editor Lynne Smith, who picked up the odd mistake; and to Niki Savva for checking context. My special thanks go to Australia's pre-eminent political satirist Geoff Pryor for his drawings and cartoons, and for the fun in collating them. I am indebted to the late Tracey Aubin for her encouragement and enthusiasm. My thanks to Sir James Killen, one of the few politicians who was also a true parliamentarian, for writing the Foreword.

I am grateful to all those who have written about this 1961–2002 period in Australian politics before me. Books on which I have drawn generally for perspective include: *Robert Menzies: A Life*, by AW Martin; *RG Menzies: A Portrait*, by Sir John Bunting; *Black Jack McEwen* by Peter Golding; *The Gorton Experiment*, by Alan Reid; *Crash Through or Crash* by Laurie Oakes; *A Certain Grandeur*, by Graham Freudenberg; *The Whitlam Government*, by EG Whitlam; *Killen: Inside Australian Politics*, by Sir James Killen; *Malcolm Fraser PM*, by Patrick Weller; *Hayden*, by WG Hayden; *Hawke's Memoirs*, by Bob Hawke; *A True*

ACKNOWLEDGMENTS

Believer: Paul Keating, by Michael Gordon; and *From Curtin to Hawke,* by Fred Daly.

My primary sources have been my own notes, my weekly newspaper columns and other articles and documents which I have accumulated over these four decades.

FOREWORD

It was in 1926 that the then editor of *The Manchester Guardian,* C.P. Scott, writing about journalists said: 'Comment is free but facts are scarce'.

There have been a notable few journalists who meticulously embraced that advice. There have been a large number, alas, who have spurned it and treated it with contempt.

In my time I have known many hundreds of journalists and I unhesitatingly assert that Wallace Brown was outstanding in his regard for facts. Yes, of course, there were occasions when his journalism challenged the abiding link between truth and political stability. Whenever that happened the issue was raised with him and there was an appropriate retraction and apology. Both reflected a sense of elegance and a strong sense of propriety.

In the history of this country very few journalists have walked through the time space of ten Prime Ministers as has Wallace Brown. There were occasions when he disagreed with some of them, but his disagreement was expressed with grace and felicity. In my experience he never breached a solitary confidentiality and his respect for sensitive briefings was immaculate.

The Prime Ministers of whom he has written knew him well and to a man, they all had a respect for him that was as massive as it was unique. None of the Prime Ministers he has reflected upon ever referred to him in sharp terms of indictment.

Wallace Brown commands a unique knowledge of the political history of this country. *Ten Prime Ministers* is a singular journalistic performance. It gives an insight into facets of people which have never hitherto been considered with such authenticity. Goodwill lay behind its authorship. It is my hope that goodwill will lie behind its reception.

Sir James Killen, KCMG
Brisbane, October 2002

Preface

'Most nights are slow in the politics business,
but every once in a while you get a fast one,
a blast of wild treachery and weirdness
that even the hard boys can't handle.'

Hunter S Thompson,
Fear and Loathing on the Campaign Trail

There were two rather nervous, though outwardly confident, young newcomers to Canberra, on the TAA Fokker Friendship from Sydney that bumpy February day in 1962. One was Bill Hayden and the other was Wallace Brown.

It was two months after the most unexpectedly dramatic federal election in Australia's history and I, aged 31, had recently been appointed as *The Courier-Mail's* sole Canberra correspondent, on trial, by one of Australia's greatest editors, TC Bray. I had been in this posting since soon after the election in December 1961 and had just been back in Brisbane for a few days of succinct de-briefing and re-briefing by Bray.

Ex-police constable Hayden, aged 28, had just surprised everybody in the political world, including himself and the dominant Robert Menzies, by winning the Ipswich-Brisbane Valley seat of Oxley for the Labor Party from long-time Liberal incumbent and popular local GP, Dr Donald

1

Cameron. Oxley, then encompassing many rural centres as well as the industrial-mining city of Ipswich, had not been held by Labor since 1906.

I had been flung into the deep end of that extraordinary political pool whose ever-encircling predatory swimmers include MPs, public servants, lobbyists, spin-doctors, diplomats and journalists. Hayden was about to attend his first Labor Party caucus meeting as a lowly Opposition backbencher under the critical eyes of the veteran and often acerbic leader Arthur Calwell and his deputy Gough Whitlam.

Hayden even then was noted for his brashness, but as we walked across the Canberra Airport tarmac into the small wooden terminal building that sufficed for a national capital of only 50 000 people, he said: 'Wally, I think you'll last a bit longer here than I will.'

It had been an extraordinary, historic and even symbolic election. Menzies and his Liberal-Country Party Coalition Government, which had been in office for 12 years and was presiding over a basically comfortable and prosperous Australia (even though unemployment had reached a post-war high of 2 per cent!) had found its majority cut from 32 to two—that is, one on the floor of the House of Representatives after providing a Speaker.

The Government had survived by this narrowest of margins only because a majority of Communist preferences had gone quirkily to ardent anti-Communist Jim Killen in the Brisbane seat of Moreton. The founder of the Country Party, Earle Page, had died a week after election day at the age of 81. Whitlam had made his mark as a campaigner, particularly in Queensland, and reinforced his credentials as a future Labor leader. Left-winger Lionel Murphy, the person who later was to become responsible above all others for the development of the sweeping parliamentary committee system, had won a Senate seat in New South Wales. This seat was for a Labor

2

Party whose firm written policy was to abolish the Senate.

Hayden himself, lampooned early in his parliamentary career by Menzies as a 'little ignoramus', went on to be the best Labor leader never to become prime minister, foreign minister and at his own request, Governor-General.

Said Menzies with candour, after he finally surfaced from personal gloom and apprehension to hold a press conference 10 days after the election: 'What a dumper!'

Looking back across 40 years of national politics, over the administrations and impact of 10 prime ministers, over 17 election campaigns, it is a mistake to become overly nostalgic. It is important, however, and maybe even enlightening, to remember some of the genuine wit, to lament the drop in parliamentary standards, to note the changes in the media and its coverage of politics, and to record the gradual but still difficult rise of women in public life.

In 1902, Australia may have been one of the first countries to have given women the right to vote (the first State was South Australia in 1894), but 60 years later in 1962 there were only two women in federal Parliament: Senators Dorothy Tangney of Western Australia and Annabelle Rankin of Queensland. By 1999, there were 53 women—21 Senators and 32 members of the House of Representatives; and by July 2002, there were 61 female federal MPs—23 Senators and 38 members of the House of Representatives. This was 27 per cent of the total, but women were still seriously under-represented on the frontbenches of the major parties, either in government or opposition. The glass ceiling remains.

It is important also to note the significant sweep of history and policy changes over those 40 years.

In 1961, Australian people still lived in the wake of World War II. They harboured a fear of a militarily resurgent Japan and they were grateful to have the umbrella of the ANZUS Pact, which that latent fear had inspired in 1954. Yet by 1992, the change in the official Australian attitude had become so marked that Paul Keating told a Tokyo audience Australia would do nothing that harmed Japan's interests in the Pacific region.

At the turn of the century even the value of the American military alliance was being questioned by some erstwhile unquestioning allies, including Malcolm Fraser. Then nine months into the 21st century, the government led by John Howard put Australia unequivocably in the American camp again, even activating the ANZUS Treaty in response to the terrorist attacks on New York and Washington.

In 1961, there was an atmosphere of innocence, peace and security for Australian's on their island continent. There were no gross acts of wanton terrorism against them, at home or abroad. On 12 October 2002, came the horror of the Bali bombing.

In 1961, Australians were still British subjects and the Privy Council was their highest court of appeal. It was not until 1973 they became wholly-Australian citizens, and 1986, when the Australia Act was passed by the British Parliament, that appeals to the Privy Council from the States as well as the Commonwealth were abolished.

In 1961 an Englishman, Lord de L'Isle, was Australia's Governor-General, resident at Yarralumla. In 1999 a referendum on a republic failed, but only because the majority of Australians who favoured a republic could not agree on its formulation.

In 1961, this nation still had a White Australia policy and it was left to Harold Holt's administration to start to abolish it. Later, Gough Whitlam scrapped it as policy in a Labor Party that had introduced it before Federation in the Chinese gold rush days and federally in 1902.

In 1961, the population of 13.5 million was

4

predominantly of British or Irish origins. Ninety per cent of Australians had been born in Australia, Britain or Ireland. By 1971, the British immigrants had fallen from 73 per cent to 42 per cent of the total intake. By 2002, the population was 19.5 million, 25 per cent had been born overseas, 10 per cent were of non-European origin, and 4 million people had at least one parent who had been born overseas. Twenty-five per cent of the Foreign Affairs and Trade Department officers had been born overseas or born in Australia of non-Australian parents.

In 1961, there was no Commonwealth government involvement in education. Menzies changed that forever when he directly boosted funds for universities and gave state aid to private schools.

In 1961, there was no national health scheme. Whitlam changed that with Medibank, later superceded by Medicare.

In 1961, financial regulations decreed that banks had to hold statutory reserves with the Commonwealth (reserve) Bank and that life insurance companies had to hold at least 30 per cent of assets in government and semi-government securities. The Labor Party was actively promoting its age-old policy of socialisation of the means of production, distribution and exchange. The basic philosophy of all parties was that tariff protection was needed to safeguard Australian industries.

In the 1980s and 1990s and even into the new century, the anachronistic socialisation plank was still officially a Labor tenet. But it was the Labor administration of Bob Hawke, with Keating as Treasurer, that floated the dollar and privatised the Commonwealth Bank, TAA, and the Commonwealth Serum Laboratories. At the start of the 21st century both major parties extolled the virtues of free trade and globalisation.

Politics is people as well as policies, and four groups of people generally run Australia. These are: the elected

Federal Government (meaning in effect and in most circumstances the Prime Minister and the Treasurer); the appointed Commonwealth bureaucracy (meaning in effect and in most circumstances the Secretaries of the Prime Minister's Department and the Treasury); the appointed High Court (meaning the Chief Justice and other judges); and the appointed Reserve Bank Board (meaning in effect and in most circumstances the Governor). Sometimes, rarely, there is a fifth person who moves in: the appointed Governor-General. It is the constant interaction between all these people that constitutes the essential dynamic of the administration of Australia.

To complete the picture, to these must be added the media in all forms—big newspapers, small newsletters, radio and television—but particularly the reporters, the commentators, the cartoonists and other satirists, and the photographers. They provide the necessary reflective, reactive and recording link between the politicians and the people.

This account however is mainly about the 10 Prime Ministers in the last half of the 20th century and the start of the 21st century and their methods, idiosyncrasies, personalities and impact:

1.   Robert Menzies, the most accomplished politician and parliamentarian.
2.   Harold Holt, a most courteous and capable lieutenant who had spent too long in Menzies' shade.
3.   John McEwen, the most single-minded and strong-willed.
4.   John Gorton, the first modern Australian nationalist larrikin in the job.
5.   William McMahon, the most disappointing.
6.   Gough Whitlam, the most innovative, self-confident and erratic.
7.   Malcolm Fraser, the most controversial and complex.

8. Bob Hawke, the most egotistical but a good chairman of the board.
9. Paul Keating, the savage big-picture man who liked to live dangerously.
10. John Howard, the most conservative, and the most tenacious, underestimated survivor.

It has been my privilege to have been in personal contact with, reported on, commented about, and travelled with, these 10 Prime Ministers.

In news reporting and 2000 weekly newspaper columns by me over this period, the perceived proper objective has been to be objective. Many other people of course have written about these times, events and people with great authority and expertise: to name a few, politicians such as Menzies, Whitlam, Hawke, Hayden, John Button and Sir James Killen; bureaucrats such as Sir John Bunting; journalists such as Alan Reid, Paul Kelly, Laurie Oakes and David Solomon; speechwriters such as Graham Freudenberg and Don Watson; academics such as Professor Clem Lloyd and Patrick Weller. No book is more impressive and scholarly than the academic AW Martin's two-volume *Robert Menzies: A Life*.

This is one reporter's condensed subjective view and recollections. Hopefully, some details are filled in and there is some wisdom of hindsight. Much of it has been stranger than fiction. Most of it has been great fun.

And Bill Hayden's prediction of 40 years ago came true. I have, after all, lasted longer in Canberra than him. The wheel of circumstance turned full circle in 1995, when shortly before he retired as Governor-General, he wrote a note: 'Wal has more puff power than me.'

Menzies

KEEPING IT SIMPLE

**Robert Gordon Menzies, Liberal
(1939–41 & 1949–66)
18 years, 5 months and 12 days.**

'You should have been given an Oscar, not a Thistle.'
Labor MP Jim Fraser (ACT) in the House of Representatives,
April 1963

'Above all, he was a fascinating, generous, affectionate man who yet found time for a certain amount of hearty intolerance and well-selected hatreds.'
Sir Lionel Lindsay

In the wake of his Liberal-Country Party Government's startling near-defeat in the general election of December 1961, Robert Menzies, aged 67 that month, was, briefly, a chastened man, though few would have known it from his public manner when Parliament resumed in February of 1962.

Menzies and his Coalition had been lucky to have survived at all. There were 124 members of the House of Representatives at that time, of which 122 represented electorates within the six States and had full voting rights. Of these 122 seats, Menzies and his Coalition had 62 to Labor's 60 (which gave the Coalition its majority of one on the floor of the House after providing a Speaker). The other two members represented the Australian Capital Territory and the Northern Territory and they were both Labor Members. But they did not have full voting rights in those days. They could vote only on legislation that specifically affected their constituencies. If they had been allowed full voting rights, the Liberal-Country Party Coalition and Labor would have levelled out at 62-all. The state of play, politics and parties may well have been markedly different. At best, Menzies would have been leader of a minority government after providing a Speaker. At worst for him, the Governor-General (Viscount de L'Isle, the last of the British Vice-Regal incumbents) may have called on Labor leader Arthur Calwell to have tried to form a government, since the ALP had won a majority of votes.

None of which pointless 'if-only' hypothesis worried Menzies when Eddie Ward, the acerbic Left-wing Labor MP for East Sydney and one of Parliaments great debaters, fired the first question at him. 'Is it a fact', Ward asked, 'that the Prime Minister received a congratulatory message from Mr Khruschev, the Russian leader, on the re-election? Did the Prime Minister in his reply express his pleasure and appreciation at the success of the unity ticket between the Liberals and the Communists and especially thank him for the 95 Communist preference votes in the Moreton electorate without which his Government would have been defeated?'

Menzies was watched closely by tense Liberal backbenchers, and not least by Jim Killen. Incidentally, contrary to the well-publicised story that Menzies had congratulated him on his vital narrow survival in Moreton with the words: 'Killen, you are magnificent', in fact he had merely been told by Menzies on the phone: 'Well laddie, this is good news. I'm glad it's over.'

Replied Menzies smoothly to Ward, in part: 'My reply will have none of the charm of novelty. I did not have a message of that kind from Mr Khruschev. I did hear a rumour that he was inquiring for the address of the honourable member for East Sydney'. The laughter on all sides that followed, much of it at Killen's expense as well as Ward's, immediately restored Menzies' political abilities in the minds of his Coalition colleagues.

This is my basic point. The Menzies I knew in the 1960s was a consummate politician and parliamentarian, nothing less and rather more. In the Canberra of that era he was approaching the end of his long career but he was still a larger-than-life figure, ruling his colleagues with wit, admonishing finger, raised eyebrow, sophistication and a talent for simplification. Behind him were many milestones.

There was his brilliant legal career as an advocate. His first period as prime minister at the start of World War II. His popularity in Britain at that time. His resignation from the leadership of the (pre-Liberal) United Australia Party because of lack of support and his apparent subsequent descent towards oblivion. His landmark speech on 'The Forgotten People, the middle class' in the second half of 1942. His formation of the Liberal Party in meetings at

Canberra and Albury in 1944. His triumphant return to power in 1949 with Country Party leader Arthur Fadden as his junior Coalition partner.

Domestically, significant events included his exploitation of the great split in the Labor Party in the 1950s. His notorious clashes with the brilliant and eccentric Labor leader Dr HV Evatt. His failure, largely due to Evatt's opposition, to make the Communist Party an illegal body.

His condemnation, with Evatt's and especially Arthur Calwell's support, of journalist Frank Browne of the *Bankstown Observer* and its proprietor Ray Fitzpatrick. In that infamous case in 1955, the Government (and Parliament) were prosecutor, jury and judge and sent the two men to Goulburn jail for three months for breach of parliamentary privilege. The House of Representatives Privileges Committee had reported that the *Bankstown Observer* had deliberately tried to discredit and silence a Labor backbencher, Charles Morgan, by imputing he was corrupt. Though the Clerk of the House, Frank Green, advised that there had been no breach of privilege, Menzies moved that Browne and Fitzpatrick be jailed. Evatt moved an amendment that they be fined instead, but lost this on a division.

The Petrov Affair of 1954, in which Soviet diplomat Vladimir Petrov, an officer of the MVD (the Soviet Ministry of State Security), defected from his Embassy in Canberra into the arms of the Australian Security Intelligence Organisation (ASIO), sought and was granted political asylum, and brought with him information about espionage in Australia. It was a dramatic event made more so by Menzies' announcement of a Royal Commission to investigate Petrov's documents; by the forcible disarming at Darwin Airport of Soviet guards who were taking Petrov's wife back to Russia, which allowed her also to seek political asylum; by the antagonism, and even paranoia of Dr Evatt; and by an impending election.

Other milestones included his government's initiation of an innovative forward-thinking foreign policy measure—the Colombo Plan—which led to hundreds of future decision makers in Asia gaining their higher education in Australia. It was a plan which, in its final wording, had been drafted by a young External Affairs officer (who later became the last true public service mandarin), Arthur Tange, on the seven-hour flight from Singapore to Colombo in January 1950.

In foreign policy also: the Australia-Japan Trade Agreement; Menzies' commitment of troops to the Korean War; the ANZUS and SEATO Pacts.

And his failed excursions into international affairs such as Suez (in which he did not take into account the surge of Egyptian nationalism) and South Africa's withdrawal from the Commonwealth (in which he urged Britain not to support a UN condemnation of apartheid).

Despite his huge reputation and popularity among conservatives in Britain and the US, he had a terse relationship with India's beloved Pandit Nehru, within the context of both the (former British) Commonwealth and the UN Assembly, and Nehru occasionally got the better of him.

In the serious Cold War days of October of 1960, for instance, when I was in New York as a representative of *The Courier-Mail*, at a special heads-of-government session at the UN, I watched an extraordinary session. The USSR's Nikita Khruschev thumped his shoe on the rostrum, then Menzies made a speech on South Africa and apartheid that totally backed the British and US position, then the neutralist Nehru savagely attacked Menzies' logic.

As a result, a particular amendment by Menzies to a five-power resolution was voted down. Some of the

Australian press reported that Australia had been humiliated, while in the lobbies of the UN building on New York's East Side, the perception among many bemused delegates was that between them Menzies and Nehru had managed to split the Commonwealth.

In those days, security surrounding Australian prime ministers was virtually non-existent and contact between this particular Australian correspondent and Menzies was not difficult. As I walked part of the way back across Manhattan with Menzies and his small group of staffers and advisers, and one bodyguard, that night—he to the Waldorf Astoria, me to the (Melbourne) *Herald & Weekly Times* office in the New York Times building—his language about Nehru was blunt. Nehru's attack, he said, had been poisonous, primitive and too clever by half. This was accepted as strict 'off-the-record' time. I took no notes. Nothing was printed. Indeed, much of it was unprintable anyway.

In 1962, though the fine domestic political balance was the backdrop to Menzies' stage, foreign policy remained the big issue. The focus was on, meaning against, Britain's application to join the European Economic Community. For some months a still-lethargic Menzies, who had relinquished the External Affairs portfolio to Sir Garfield Barwick, left Australia's running on Britain's application to his Coalition partner, Country Party leader and Trade Minister John McEwen. More accurately, the redoubtable McEwen beat him to the start line and by March was in London railing against Britain's move.

Though Menzies had privately raised his concerns with the British about the effect on his beloved Commonwealth, suddenly it was McEwen who was publicly raising the spectre of the end of old Empire trade preferences and the effect on Australian exports to Britain. This was a nuts and bolts approach, which appealed to Australians, and because

Menzies was being over-shadowed, there was a push within sections of the Liberal Party for McEwen to become prime minister. Victorian Sir Wilfrid Kent Hughes, who was never enamoured of Menzies, was a particular McEwen fan.

McEwen did nothing to discourage this. In one background interview with me (and no doubt separately with other members of the small Press Gallery) he made the point that though he could never join the Liberal Party there was a precedent for a Country Party leader (Fadden in 1941) to become prime minister at the request of the Liberal Party. McEwen, however, did not disparage Menzies. He merely said some Liberals who had approached him had observed that Menzies seemed to be tiring in the job.

Menzies, however, was fortunate to have as press secretary a gregarious mixer in former *Sydney Morning Herald* journalist Ray Maley, who quickly, and mainly in the Non-Members Bar at Old Parliament House, picked up McEwen's clever ploy. Maley reported to Menzies. At the same time the Liberal Party federal executive met to discuss McEwen's apparent bid and called on State branches to close ranks. Menzies got the message. He pulled himself out of his post-election trough, rose to the challenge, took off quickly for Europe in May, took over where McEwen had left off, and in a series of speeches that were hailed by the British establishment, regained the lead role in defending Australia's position and condemning the pro-Europeans headed by Edward Heath. Menzies was back in control and McEwen knew it.

By the time Menzies called a premature House of Representatives election in November 1963, he had returned to his peak domestically. It was to be his last electoral triumph, and it was a personal one, rivalling his second coming in 1949. This time he left nothing to chance.

In foreign and defence policy he had ordered (at what

turned out to be big and escalating expense) revolutionary folding-wing F-111 bombers from the USA, with the clear implication they could reach Jakarta if necessary.

He had also been handed a bonus by his opponents in the form of a special ALP Federal Conference held at Canberra's Hotel Kingston to decide party policy on a US Naval Communications base proposed by his government at North West Cape in Western Australia. Ridiculous Labor rules at that time excluded the party's parliamentary leaders from taking part in a Conference. Calwell and Whitlam were photographed (by Peter Hardacre of *The Daily Telegraph,* Sydney) outside the Kingston as they waited forlornly late at night for the 36 delegates inside to make a decision. Alan Reid tagged them 'the 36 faceless' men in *The Daily Telegraph* and Menzies latched on to this devastating catchphrase.

When it came to domestic issues, Menzies chose his time well and shamelessly seized on little bits of his opponents' policy, exploiting Labor divisions in the process.

In the 1961 election, unemployment, a credit squeeze and his relatively tight Budget policy had been the main issues. But this time Menzies and Treasurer Harold Holt did a 180 degrees switch to deficit financing (which had been advocated by Labor in 1961) in the Budget of August 1962, with a record deficit of 118 million pounds. By August 1963, unemployment had dropped to 1.5 per cent and there were all of 67 229 registered jobseekers! This was the lowest since the boom days of 1960.

As well, there was the issue of state (meaning government) aid to non-government schools, which was the cause of much blood-letting in a Labor Party still reeling from the partly sectarian split of the 1950s. The New South Wales Labor Government led by Premier RJ Heffron had budgeted to provide grants to non-government schools to build science blocks. But an ALP federal Conference in Perth had carried a resolution which in effect opposed state aid, and the 12-man federal executive denounced Heffron's decisions as violation of Labor policy.

Menzies waited no longer. He again projected himself not just as the friend of big business but the champion of Middle Australia. He called the election in November, seeking a mandate of government stability. Without consulting the Liberal Party, he promised to give 5 million pounds to both State government and non-government schools to build science blocks. Catholics cheered. Arthur Calwell, ironically a papal knight, shuddered (and when the relevant legislation subsequently was introduced, said angrily: 'This bill was conceived in chicanery, born in duplicity and nurtured on deceit'). The Rightist Democratic Labor Party, that breakaway body which formed during the great Labor split and comprising many Catholics, backed Menzies and campaigned fiercely on the dangers of communism within and without.

There was one other factor. Menzies was perceived by many in the ALP, including Fred Daly and Calwell, to have been helped by the assassination of US President John Kennedy eight days before polling day. Calwell, the grandson of an American, wept over breakfast in Perth and later in Geraldton (WA) when he heard the news. He heard a garbled version of a comment by Menzies, and against the advice of his staff issued a dramatic but inaccurate one-liner: 'Menzies has smeared the blood of the ALP over the coffin of a dead president'. Calwell was worried, correctly, that Australian voters would be less inclined to change governments at such a time.

Whatever the specific or combined reasons, when the votes came in, the Coalition Government's majority had risen from two to 22. Much to Arthur Calwell's chagrin, the

Liberals picked up five seats in metropolitan Sydney.

There was a fascinating sidelight in the run-up to the campaign, which reflected Menzies' ambivalent attitude to the press. He tended to court proprietors (with the exception of the Fairfax clan at *The Sydney Morning Herald*, who he never forgave for their support of the ALP in 1961) and confide with editors but not seriously with journalists in the Press Gallery.

TC (later Sir Theodor) Bray, long-time editor of *The Courier-Mail*, never failed to seek an appointment with Menzies each time he came to Canberra and Menzies never failed to grant an audience. In October of 1963, there was considerable speculation in the Press Gallery that Menzies would call an early election. But none of it was informed, until Bray came out of a private meeting with Menzies and said to me: 'If I were you, I'd wait until this time next week and write that he is planning on an election late in November.' This I duly did. Menzies announced the election two days later. A congratulatory telex message came from Bray, by then safely back in Brisbane, saying drily: 'You obviously have some good sources'.

One Gallery journalist of whom Menzies was fond was Jack Fingleton, former opening Test batsman for Australia. But this was because Menzies liked to talk about cricket, one of his greatest loves. He wrote a foreword for one of Fingleton's books on cricket, could occasionally be found yarning to Fingleton in the parliamentary library, and once delayed resumption of a Loan Council meeting while so engaged.

Menzies' rapport with Fingleton was in stark contrast to his relationship with Ian Fitchett, a Falstaffian figure and former distinguished war correspondent who wrote first for *The Age* (in Melbourne) and then *The Sydney Morning Herald*. It was Fitchett who called Menzies 'Ming the Merciless' after a cartoon character and he could occasionally match Menzies in the art of repartee. When *The Sydney Morning Herald* switched to supporting Calwell in 1961, Menzies was particularly angry at an article Fitchett had written, and when crossing King's Hall that day, passed Fitchett and some colleagues yarning across a common meeting ground, Queen Victoria's table (on which she had signed the proclamation which brought the Commonwealth of Australia into existence). Snapped Menzies: 'I'll make you eat crow, Fitchett. I'll have your guts for garters.' Retorted Fitchett: 'As long as they are garnished with the sauce of your embarrassment, Prime Minister.'

For the most part, and sometimes with reason, Menzies barely tolerated many journalists. On one occasion he was greeted at Sydney Airport after a long flight across the Pacific Ocean by a young reporter seeking an interview. The reporter began: 'Mr Menzies, I am from the Sydney *Mirror*', Menzies replied: 'My boy, you have my deepest sympathy', and strode past.

But he tended to respect most members of the Press Gallery, then numbering about 47, even if he did not like them, and when Parliament was not sitting he generally announced any important development or policy at a press conference with the Gallery. When Parliament was sitting, he correctly, and in contrast to most of his successors, made any announcement there.

One such announcement he made was on a pay rise his Government had approved for MPs. He came under concerted attack for several days from editors and Press Gallery journalists. He dismissed them all (and proceeded with the pay rise, much to the agreement of all MPs) with lofty disdain in a subsequent speech to the House: 'Gentlemen (there were no women members of the House of Representatives at the time), who are we to have running this country, the Government or this man Henderson

[Rupert Henderson, managing director of *The Sydney Morning Herald*]? Who are we to have in control, the Parliament or the press?'

Though they often criticised him and disliked his (surprisingly-shy) aloofness, Canberra journalists in return showed their respect for Menzies as politician and parliamentarian when, on 21 September 1964, they gave him a special National Press Club luncheon to mark the 30th anniversary of his entry into the House of Representatives. This was before the National Press Club had its own premises and the function was held at the old Hotel Canberra, where the manager, Thornley Thorpe, greeted him at the entrance with a martini of frightening size and where, at his request, the main dish on the menu was Irish stew.

In retrospect, given that parliamentary debate as he knew it is no more, the most interesting observation he made at that lunch was on its great virtues: 'The whole glory of parliamentary debate is that it is cut and thrust,' he said. 'Parliamentary debate is the clash of minds. It is the debate, which swerves from one side to the other under the pressure of events, which accommodates itself in a new argument, a new thought. This is the most fascinating thing in the world...'

That also was a day which showed Menzies displaying his full physical and intellectual stamina. For after the celebratory lunch came Question Time in the House, which he handled with his expected finesse; then I next saw him at a diplomatic cocktail party at about 5 pm, where he downed his customary martini. Later he was guest speaker at a dinner back at the Hotel Canberra; then he was in the House of Representatives at 8 pm listening to a speech by McEwen; then he chaired a Cabinet meeting (and probably had a few post-Cabinet drinks). At about 1 am as I was leaving the building, I saw him departing, carrying his big frame quite steadily across the frosty grass to his Commonwealth car.

Because he was a whale among minnows (with the exception of McEwen) in the Coalition, and because the Liberal Party endowed him, as (wrongly, in my view) it does all its leaders, with immense and often dictatorial powers of patronage, and because his personality was so strong, his style of administration was essentially personal.

Arthur Calwell is a tad apprehensive as Menzies limbers up at Question Time.

Sometimes, however, it was delightfully so. Only Menzies, for instance, with his urbanity and immense powers of advocacy, could have persuaded Sir Donald Bradman to come out of 15 years of retirement to captain the Prime Ministers' Eleven in its traditional carnival-type match against the visiting England cricket team at Manuka Oval in Canberra in February 1963. Never before or since has there been such public excitement or anticipation at such a game. Bradman made one scoring shot, a typical offside boundary, and then was out for four. As Menzies later recalled in his *The Measure of the Years*: 'Poor Brian Statham (the bowler) was most dejected. The umpire should have no-balled him, for the common good.' Still, Manuka Oval had a record crowd and Legacy collected record proceeds.

Menzies' style could also be idiosyncratic, with a sense of humour. More often than not, he would amuse himself (but not some of his more nervous colleagues) at Question Time by pulling out a plain piece of paper, drawing lines across, and marking what appeared to be a score card on his ministers' performances. At the end of Question Time he would always deliberately fold and tear this score sheet into tiny pieces and, grinning and raising an eyebrow, drop it into the wastepaper basket, so that nobody ever knew what his assessment was. He was a master in the little theatre of Parliament, though because he relied on timing and inflection his wit could seldom be captured properly in print.

In slightly more serious vein, I once happened to be privy to a fascinating conversation in the government lobby between Menzies and Holt, the result of which was the splendid National Library as we now know it on the shore of Lake Burley Griffin.

For years, Sir Harold White, who was both Parliamentary Librarian and National Librarian, but whose only library was the one in Old Parliament House, had been pressing the Government to build a proper national library. For the same period, Holt, ever a treasurer with a tight grip on the nation's purse strings, had ignored White's overtures. White was a short man in stature, with two main characteristics: persistence and incessant, unstoppable verbiage. On this particular occasion, I was leaving my office late at night and was going down the stairs to the corridor leading to King's Hall. Out of the Prime Minister's suite in the corner of the building came first White, rapidly and alone, and about 20 paces behind him and slowly, Menzies and Holt.

Menzies turned and nodded in recognition as I walked several paces behind and the PM and his Treasurer continued on their way. Said Menzies to Holt: 'For God's sake, Harold, give him his bloody library and get him off my back.' As White continued on into the night through King's Hall, Menzies and Holt turned into Holt's office (possibly for a nightcap!) and as I walked past, Menzies nodded to me again, said nothing and winked. I wrote a story the next day on an expected Government decision to build a national library. Such was the beauty of that small, cramped, uncomfortable, democratic and efficient Old Parliament House!

Menzies' personal style, however, could also be autocratic. He largely ignored some highly intelligent, albeit eccentric, Liberal backbenchers such as Billy (self-styled William Charles the Fourth) Wentworth, whose most significant contribution was to head a parliamentary committee which finally forced standardisation of railways on the nation. Sir Wilfrid Kent Hughes, who had briefly been a minister, privately would refer to Menzies as 'Banyan Tree Bob', because in his shade he would allow nothing to grow. Joe Gullett, former distinguished soldier, able MP and Government Whip and later Ambassador to Greece, but never a minister, always admired Menzies immense powers of persuasion but used to say Menzies often treated his backbenchers with ill-concealed condescension.

Menzies had a deliberate habit of generally not slotting experts in their fields into matching portfolios, with the marked exception of his own field, the law. His Attorney-General of necessity was always a lawyer and often a most distinguished one, such as Sir Garfield Barwick (who he persuaded to enter Parliament in 1958 as a possible alternative to Harold Holt as his successor). But Menzies often caused much rumbling in Coalition ranks with other allocations of portfolios. His backbenchers regarded it as strange, to say the least, that his Army Minister for years was Sir John Cramer, a former Sydney real estate agent, and not someone like Gullett or Country Party MP Colonel Charles Anderson, a Victoria Cross winner in the Malaya campaign in World War II.

Having resisted calls for him for years to appoint an Australian ambassador to Ireland, when Menzies eventually did so he chose a Scot, former Social Security Minister and Country Party MP Hugh Roberton! Other Ministers said there had been considerable chuckling over drinks in the Cabinet anteroom at what Menzies regarded as the rather delightful irony of inflicting a Scotsman on the Irish. Though he went to England many times as prime minister, Menzies never visited Ireland.

The 1960s of course were different times.

It was on 18 February 1963, in King's Hall that Menzies, ever the ardent monarchist, welcomed Queen Elizabeth with the famous quotation taken from an old 17th century poet who wrote: 'I did but see her passing by, and yet I shall love her till I die.' He was not seriously criticised or lampooned at the time for saying this.

It was three weeks later that the Queen made him a Knight of the Thistle as a personal honour, second only to the Order of the Garter in the old imperial honours system. It was in 1964 that he advocated in Cabinet that the basic unit of Australia's proposed new decimal currency be called a 'Royal' (but fortunately was talked out of this, reportedly mainly by Holt).

It was in mid-1965 that British (Labour) Prime Minister Harold Wilson recommended to the Queen that in succession to Sir Winston Churchill, he be made Lord

Warden of the Cinque Ports. This was the centuries-old ceremonial appointment bestowed on a person of massive authority who would be responsible for the defence against the French of the five main ports, including Dover, along the English Channel. Menzies was duly inducted, with much pomp, at Dover Castle.

Honours aside, the Cold War was still the biggest overriding factor in foreign policy. The Petrov Affair was very recent history. It was followed in 1963 by the expulsion from Australia of one of Petrov's successors, Ivan Skripov, for spying (for, among other things, according to External Affairs Minister Sir Garfield Barwick, seeking details of the proposed US Naval communications base at North West Cape).

Menzies was a proponent of the atomic bomb. He not only encouraged the British to conduct their tests at Woomera and the Monte Bello Islands, but also believed it was 'dangerous to have a nuclear-free zone in the Southern Hemisphere'. He sent troops to Malaysia to help in the successful fight against the local Communist insurgents.

His best-known simplification, and, in retrospect, mistaken assessment, of a strategic situation was his description of the Vietnam War as the 'downward thrust of Communist China between the Indian and Pacific Oceans.' He placed Australia's faith in its 'two great and powerful friends'—Britain and the USA—but had relatively little influence on either.

He could not stop the winds of change when Britain pulled back its forces from east of Suez, he could not persuade the USA to intervene to stop the Indonesian annexation/invasion of the Netherlands-held West New Guinea, and he could not persuade the USA to actively side with Australia to help Malaysia and Singapore against Sukarno-inspired Indonesian military confrontation. Then, as now, it was not in the US national interest to offend

Indonesia and it would not do so.

When it came to the USA putting pressure on Australia, however, it was a different matter, because the ANZUS and SEATO Pacts were seen, correctly in that era, as the cornerstone of defence and foreign policy. The much-vaunted US alliance had to be preserved above all else, and the great majority of Australians agreed. With his ease of simplification he persuaded them. Though the small print of both the ANZUS and SEATO Pacts made it clear the USA was not committed to come automatically to Australia's aid in time of conflict, Menzies invariably managed to make out that it was, and it was against this background that Australia went into the Vietnam War.

In hindsight, this ill-fated divisive commitment and its nasty corollary — selective national conscription under a system of birthday ballot among men turning 20 — were the biggest negatives of Menzies' career, but it has to be remembered that most Australians went along with them initially.

Announcement of the birthday ballot came in November of 1964, when Menzies said Australia had to prepare for 'a deterioration in our strategic position' in the SEATO area. In Parliament he referred to Indonesia's confrontationist actions against Malaysia, the growth of communism in Laos and South Vietnam, and the possibility of Indonesian incursions from West Irian into Papua New Guinea, then still an Australian colony. Inevitably this was an issue in a half-Senate election a few weeks later, which left the Coalition without a majority in the upper House but with assured support from a Democratic Labor Party that had campaigned blatantly against Red threats and Yellow perils.

The beginning of Australia's Vietnam commitment was as far back as 1962, when 10 Army instructors were sent to assist in counter-insurgency and jungle-fighting training.

ROBERT MENZIES

Their numbers were gradually increased over the next three years, until April 1965, when Menzies announced Australia would send an infantry battalion to take part directly in the conflict. Though the Australian Government said this battalion was being sent in response to a request from the Government of South Vietnam, and though the South Vietnam Government itself said so on April 29, this is not borne out by the evidence of the relevant documents.

Professor RG Neale, official Foreign Affairs Department historian and subsequently Government Archivist, produced a detailed paper in 1975 in which he found Australian military assistance to South Vietnam was not at any time in response to a request for defence aid from South Vietnam as a protocol state to SEATO. Neale reported that the requests for aid were largely generated by the USA, which did not actually need military help but wanted to show the world it was not alone in its efforts against communism in South-East Asia. Neale also concluded that the Menzies Government had decided to provide military aid for political reasons to ensure its long-term defence interests were upheld. These interests being forward defence against communism in the region and the need to retain US commitment of power to the Asian area, 'thus to commit her to a practical guarantee of active support to Australia through the ANZUS and SEATO treaties.' It is now history that the USA and its allies lost the Vietnam War, that Australia's commitment reached over 8000 men, of whom 503 died.

Menzies, however, also could look back on many positives. They outweighed the negatives. Not least of his achievements was the already-mentioned Colombo Plan to help war-battered and developing Asian nations.

Menzies did not have his eyes focused only on the 'Mother Country' and the USA, for it was also his

27

Government (largely at the urging of McEwen, then Trade Minister) which signed the Australia-Japan Trade Agreement of 1957, giving Japan 'most favoured nation' status in return for import concessions. Seventeen years earlier it had been Menzies who appointed Australia's first ambassador to an Asian country: Sir John Latham to Japan in 1940. The Colombo Plan and the trade agreement with Australia's former hated wartime enemy were significant starting points in Australia's re-orientation with Asia.

But though Menzies loved the world stage, where more honours than brickbats were showered upon him, it is within Australia that he left his three biggest marks.

The first was the start of heavy Commonwealth involvement in education, hitherto regarded as the states' responsibility and prerogative. For Menzies the universities had priority and against Treasury reservations in particular in the later 1950s he established the Universities Grants Commission, which gave universities, albeit state bodies, direct access to a Commonwealth body which would deal with their financial requirements. His support for universities came from the heart. Commonwealth aid to both government and non-government secondary schools followed, initially as a deliberate political measure, in 1963. And so, from small beginnings...

The second was the development of Canberra into a place truly worthy of being the national and administrative capital. Probably only Menzies, oozing imperturbable authority and alternately persuading and ordering, could have formed the National Capital Development Commission under architect John Overall and given it the power and money to proceed. He shifted thousands of stubborn public servants from Melbourne and Sydney, proceeded with Walter Burley Griffin's plan to form an artificial lake on the meandering Molonglo River, and turned a bush town of 10 suburbs into a lovely city of which all Australians can be proud. All this was achieved in the face of significant opposition and criticism from business and electors.

In North Queensland in particular, he was hissed and booed at meetings over his plan for the Commonwealth to spend all of five million pounds on the Scrivener Dam that was to back up the water for Lake Burley Griffin. It was like water off a duck's back. His determination was clear. After one meeting at Mount Isa where he had been heavily criticised for not providing money for local sewerage works and paved roads instead, he boarded his TAA flight and with a low chuckle said to Press Secretary Ray Maley and accompanying journalists: 'When do we get back to civilisation, away from these barbarians?'

Menzies' third hallmark was his great contribution to clean government. His personal integrity was unquestioned and there was no sign of corruption in administration. He oversaw and set standards for an impartial public service, and one that did not change, American-style, with changes of government.

As a result he came to be highly respected by senior public servants, even by those who may have disagreed with some of his policies. Some later prime ministers, especially John Howard, who altered the system of senior public service employment to one of short-term contract, ignored a wise Menzies' observation. This was that in Australia the decision to provide permanent tenure for the Public Service proper had been taken to avoid the 'evils' prevalent in the US system, where a presidential election determined the fate and future of many holders of public office.

He had set the benchmark for his own impartiality in 1949. He told colleagues such as Fadden that the first thing he would do on coming into office would be to sack Roland Wilson (Secretary of the Treasury) and Dr HC ('Nugget')

Coombs (Governor of the Commonwealth Bank, at that time the central bank) because they had been the socialists advising Ben Chifley on how to establish absolute control of the Commonwealth purse strings by nationalising the banks. Upon entering office, he did no such thing. He kept them on in their jobs and they promptly advised him on how to achieve his own aim of Commonwealth control of the purse strings (for he was neither a free-marketeer nor, really, a federalist) without nationalising the banks.

He demanded loyalty from public servants, and got it. In some cases—for example, Sir John Bunting, long-time Secretary of the Prime Minister's Department, and Peter Heydon, his former private secretary who rose to become Secretary of the Immigration Department—he got virtual idolatry. In later years, Bunting used to reminisce wistfully about the value of cosy informal Sunday night gatherings at The Lodge, when Menzies would have a few of his mandarins and their wives in for drinks and dinner and discussions of current issues. His personal secretary, Hazel Craig, who also had been Ben Chifley's secretary and before that had worked for John Curtin, and who stayed with Menzies for several years after he left politics, worshipped him.

In probably the most serious episode in Australia's peacetime history, however, one of Menzies' top advisers let him down. Shortly before midnight on 10 February 1964, the destroyer HMAS *Voyager* collided with the flagship of the Royal Australian Navy, the aircraft carrier HMAS *Melbourne*, in exercises off Jervis Bay on the New South Wales coast. The Voyager was cut in half and sank with a loss of 82 lives. It was the worst accident suffered by Australia's armed services outside World Wars I and II. In Canberra, Navy headquarters headed by the Chief of the Naval Staff, Vice Admiral Sir Hastings Harrington, decided that nothing would be revealed to the public until the following day.

Fortunately, the Navy's young public relations officer, emigrant English journalist Tony Eggleton, realised such a nonsensical attempt at censorship would be counter-productive, because craft from Jervis Bay were already under way to the scene and hospitals at Nowra and Sydney had been alerted. To nip rumours and heightened public alarm in the bud, Eggleton took it upon himself to reveal the facts as he knew them. He phoned newspaper representatives in the Press Gallery one by one, and in my case, said at about 2 am: 'I hate to tell you this, but we've sunk a ship tonight... [long pause]... one of ours. It will be miraculous if there is no loss of life.' The morning newspapers naturally brought out special late editions.

Unfortunately however, Vice Admiral Harrington decided he would not disturb the Prime Minister at The Lodge. The first Menzies knew of the collision was in the morning when he heard the headline news in an ABC broadcast and read the details in *The Sydney Morning Herald.* As Bunting told me some years later: 'It was one of the few occasions on which I have known him express genuine fury. He rang me from The Lodge and shouted "Get me Harrington and get him here".' Harrington's mistake in not informing Menzies of the collision immediately, regardless of the time of night, was to have wide flow-on repercussions down the years into the regimes of Harold Holt and John Gorton.

In addition, not only did the Navy not inform Menzies immediately, it did not quickly tell next-of-kin. I had the sad experience of being phoned the next evening by the wife of one of the officers on the *Voyager*, asking if I had heard any news of her husband. I had not, but next day it was learnt that he had not survived.

In the upshot of the disaster, Menzies determined that

a normal Naval Board of Inquiry would not be sufficient, and that the 'normal naval procedures are inadequate'. He ordered a Royal Commission. It was headed by the Chief Justice of the Commonwealth Industrial Court, Sir John Spicer, and produced adverse findings (subsequently found to be basically incorrect) against Captain RJ Robertson of HMAS *Melbourne*.

Intense public debate and tense argument in Parliament followed, mainly within the Liberal Party. New South Wales Liberal MP Ted St John, a barrister, made a name for himself as an inquisitor. He also made many Liberal enemies. St John's passion for evangelical righteousness spilt into open criticism of Holt and later of Gorton in particular. In 1967, with the stress of office showing, Holt ordered a second Royal Commission. Adequate compensation for the victims of the *Voyager* disaster was still an issue 34 years later as the 21st century began.

As for Eggleton, Menzies' reaction to his unilateral tell-the-press approach on the night was favourable. For Eggleton, there was prime ministerial recognition that his actions had been justified. For him the *Voyager* episode proved to be a stepping stone. He became Menzies' press secretary after Ray Maley died suddenly—of a heart attack beside the statue of King George V in King's Hall at a reception for Princess Marina.

Menzies, who had such a general dislike of journalists, had a strange fondness for, and rapport with, his press secretaries, all of whom were former journalists. For example, Hugh Dash, who preceded Maley, was occasionally invited into the Cabinet anteroom for drinks with ministers and bureaucrats, and when Maley died in such distressing circumstances in King's Hall Menzies could not hide his anguish when he was being photographed with the Princess.

With Eggleton, a teetotaller, there was similar rapport. Shortly before he retired he invited Eggleton to join him at Kirribilli House for several days. There he confided that he was soon going to step down and as related by Eggleton years later, told him: 'There is no bigger has-been than a has-been Prime Minister'. After all he had been in that position once before, in 1941.

Eggleton, having established himself as a press secretary, went on to serve in a similar capacity with Holt, Gorton, McMahon (briefly) and Malcolm Fraser, and became federal director of the Liberal Party for 15 years and something of an elder guru in the Liberal establishment.

On 10 December 1965, 16 years to the day since the election which gave Menzies the prime ministership for the second time, he adjourned Parliament for the year. He stressed his belief in the pre-eminence of it, in what proved to be his last speech to it. The House and the Press Gallery listened in absolute silence. Arthur Calwell observed: 'I think that this occasion could be an historic one... I am proud to be here today.'

Finally, on 20 January 1966, after speculation throughout the Christmas–New Year holidays, Menzies announced his retirement. Having first informed a meeting of the parliamentary Liberal Party, he told a reasonably genial conference with the Press Gallery 'there is nothing more ex- than an ex-' and at 71 walked into retirement of his own free will while he was still in front.

He is the only prime minister to have done so. He was particularly careful not to look over Harold Holt's shoulder. He wrote his memoirs. He visited Britain. He donned his ceremonial robes as Lord Warden of the Cinque Ports. He went to the cricket. He became Chancellor of Melbourne University.

No politician has left his party in better shape, yet he

became sufficiently disillusioned with the state, policies and some candidates of the Liberals to give his first preference vote to the Democratic Labor Party in the 1969 and 1972 elections. Menzies once confided to friends: 'It is not my Liberal Party.'

He was far from rich when he retired and friends and admirers (who remained anonymous) clubbed together and raised enough money for him and Dame Pattie Menzies to buy a house in the Melbourne suburb of Malvern. After he died of a stroke in May 1978, Dame Pattie sold it and used the money to buy another one in Melbourne.

When she moved to Canberra in 1991 to be with her daughter Heather Henderson, Dame Pattie gave the money from the sale of that second house to two private girls schools in Melbourne.

Holt

THE ONE WE LOST

Harold Edward Holt, Liberal (1966–67)
1 year, 10 months and 23 days.

'Well Zara, I climbed over no-one's dead body to get here.'

Holt to his wife in January 1966

'You have an admiring friend, a staunch friend that will be all the way with LBJ.'

Holt at the White House, June 1966

No politician was groomed more assiduously for the Liberal Party leadership and prime ministership, nor worked so hard and faithfully to achieve those positions, than Harold Holt.

From the beginning of his parliamentary life in 1935 to his election unopposed by the parliamentary Liberal Party as Menzies' successor in 1966, he was a Menzies protege.

It was Menzies who brought him into the ministry of the (pre-Liberal) United Australia Party government in 1939, four years after he entered Parliament. After he enlisted in the Australian Imperial Force as a gunner in 1940, it was Menzies who asked for his release from the Army so he could rejoin the Government, following the death of three ministers (Army Minister GA Street, Air Minister JV Fairbairn and Executive Council president HS Gullett) in an RAAF aircraft crash on the approach to Canberra airport. He became Minister for Labour and when Menzies again became Prime Minister in 1949, returned to this portfolio, combining it with Immigration and then National Service.

It also was Menzies who backed Holt into the deputy Liberal leadership in 1956, in a ballot which Holt won easily and surprisingly over the veteran Richard Gardiner (later Lord) Casey, then External Affairs Minister—a ballot which some Liberal MPs saw as a payback by Menzies against Casey for disagreeing with his stand on Suez.

When Holt presented his last Budget as Treasurer to the House of Representatives in August 1965, Menzies patted him on the head, a gesture to which Holt appeared to react with more pleasure than embarrassment.

Having thus been a loyal and deferential heir-apparent to the man he affectionately described in private as 'the old man', it surprised nobody in Parliament when 'young Harold', as his mentor referred to him in return, stepped automatically into Menzies' shoes at the age of 57. His parliamentary apprenticeship had lasted 31 years and he had been deputy for 10 of them. Holt's only rival for the leadership might once have been Sir Garfield Barwick, who had been persuaded by Menzies to enter Parliament as a possible leadership contender, but by then Barwick had departed to become Chief Justice of the High Court.

Harold Holt's most endearing personal trait was his unfailing courtesy. As Treasurer he had never had a press secretary and often a knock on his door was enough for a newspaper correspondent to gain direct access without notice. Unlike Menzies, Holt had an easy and trusting relationship with regular Press Gallery journalists and he maintained this during his prime ministership.

He was greatly helped in this regard by Tony Eggleton, who he inherited as press secretary from Menzies. With justification, Eggleton regarded Holt as the prime minister he most admired personally, of all those he served. Holt was by nature a warm person. He also had charisma.

There was considerable regard and very little antagonism in the traditional love-hate politician-press relationship between Canberra Press Gallery journalists and Holt, and a good example came early, when between them they sorted out the knotty problem of which journalists should go on prime ministerial trips in VIP aircraft and who should meet the costs.

It is not generally realised that when journalists head off on trips with prime ministers in RAAF aircraft, they (or strictly, their employers) pay the full air fares, generally business class, to the Air Force. This proper system began with Holt who was the first Prime Minister to use special VIP aircraft.

The issue had not arisen with Menzies, because he had always travelled in commercial aircraft and the accompanying media people had simply paid their own way. However, Menzies had directed that two turbo-prop Vickers Viscounts be bought to form the nucleus of a VIP fleet. He had ordered British aircraft to placate the United Kingdom Government after he chose US F-111 bombers instead of British TSR-2 aircraft for the RAAF. But by the time the Viscounts arrived, Holt was in office, and the Air Force had found two second-hand ones—whose owners, ironically, had not been British. One had been owned by the Shah of Iran and the other by the Union Carbide Company of the USA.

Of the two aircraft, the Union Carbide one was slightly more luxuriously fitted out (even with space for indoor fernery!), and Holt chose it. His first overseas trip with the Viscounts (both being needed to carry advisers and the press) was to Vietnam in April 1966. He at first decided to invite selected journalists and when the Press Gallery objected to this, he responded: 'But I can do this, can't I, because the Government is paying the costs?'

The Gallery committee said: 'No, there must be no prime ministerial selection or veto. We, meaning our respective editors, will decide who goes travelling, and we, meaning our companies, will pay full expenses.' Holt, over drinks at The Lodge, eventually said: 'Okay, you're right. You decide who travels and you pay.'

Fortunately, all editors and managing directors agreed to this quite expensive deal. The result was the only appropriate one in this democracy: the prime minister of the day can demonstrate he is not seeking favours from the journalists and the journalists can show they are not beholden to the prime minister. The outcome of the Vietnam arrangements was that Holt and his advisers travelled in the Viscount formerly owned by the Union Carbide Company and the Australian press representatives chartered the Viscount formerly owned by the Shah of Iran. It was a comfortable, if slightly bizarre, way to go to look at a war.

One episode on that trip highlighted Holt's comfortable relationship with a Press Gallery that was becoming increasingly egalitarian. The first stop was Singapore and the press plane had landed first. The journalists hurried across the tarmac to the spot where Singaporean Ministers and officials were waiting beside a long red carpet to welcome Holt on his first visit as the new Australian Prime Minister. The prime ministerial RAAF Viscount duly pulled up at the end of the red carpet. With a 19-gun salute going off in the background, Holt came down the steps, ready to meet the Singaporeans. Two of the Australian journalists, Eric Walsh and Jack Allsopp, representing Sydney evening newspapers, darted in first, grabbed Holt by the hand, and laughing, said: 'Welcome to Asia, Harold!'

The Singaporeans were shocked at this intrusion. There was a deep frown from an obviously angry Holt. But then immediately came the trade-mark cover-up smile and the response: 'Hello, boys, how did you get here?' and he moved on to the official welcoming group. Later that night, having a drink with the accompanying press party, he said: 'Well, that was a little bit of fun for you. Just make sure you don't do that again to me, won't you.'

Conscious he had been in Menzies' shadow for so long, Holt quickly set out to project a different image. An Australian public accustomed to seeing Menzies in nothing but double-breasted dark suits suddenly saw pictures of Holt in a wet suit and goggles, brandishing a spear gun and emerging from the sea with two young women, his daughters-in-law, on his arms.

Holt also moved to change his image in other ways. In his first Ministry, announced on Australia Day, 1966, he included veteran Queensland Senator Dame Annabelle

Rankin as Housing Minister, the first woman to hold a portfolio in the Commonwealth Parliament (the distinction with Dame Enid Lyons being that the latter, while a Minister as vice-president of the Executive Council from 1949-51, did not administer a department). Holt also brought Malcolm Fraser, then 35, off the cold backbench and made him Army Minister.

Holt had an early test on the hustings, in a by-election in the central Queensland seat of Dawson. The seat was captured unexpectedly for the Labor Party from the Country Party by a former senior public servant, Dr Rex Patterson, who had been director of Northern Development in the National Development Department.

Though the defeat for the Coalition was felt most keenly by Country Party leader John McEwen, Holt knew he had to take some of the blame in the wake of Patterson's telling accusation that as Treasurer he had neglected the north. At the same time Holt knew that Gough Whitlam, who had campaigned tirelessly in Dawson as deputy Labor leader, was being given much of the credit, by the public and the media, for Patterson's success.

The Dawson by-election, however, made one thing abundantly clear: Harold Holt was a true Cold War warrior and a hot-war hawk on Vietnam. At a rowdy campaign meeting in Mackay he campaigned (mistakenly, as it turned out) not on regional Queensland's problems but on the perceived Communist threat from the north and the need to do everything to maintain the US alliance. It was the opening gambit of the theme he was to hone throughout 1966. It was a roller-coaster theme. In the end it was the theme that consumed him.

In keeping with this, Holt then made his own pilgrimage to Vietnam. Having been to Singapore on the way up he went to Malaysia on the way back. In both

Singapore and Malaysia, Australia's successful military and diplomatic contribution against Indonesian confrontation ensured he was particularly well received.

Indeed, this was a period in which remarkable tick-tacking through Canberra between senior Australian diplomats in Jakarta and Kuala Lumpur kept relationships afloat—at the same time as an undeclared war, in effect, was being fought. In Jakarta, the Australian Ambassador to Indonesia, KCO (Mick) Shann, had established a good professional relationship with Sukarno. Similarly, in Kuala Lumpur the Australian High Commissioner to Malaysia, Tom Critchley, had a warm relationship with Prime Minister Tunku Abdul Rahman, due partly to the fact that both were keen golfers and the High Commissioner's residence abutted the golf course on which they played together.

After a round of golf, the Tunku and Critchley generally finished up having drinks in the High Commissioner's residence where they discussed the ways of the world (and particularly of Sukarno). Critchley's reports to the Australian Government went off to Canberra where they were received by Sir Arthur Tange, then External Affairs Department Secretary. Tange sent Critchley's advice to the Australian Embassy in Jakarta, where Ambassador Shann had the ear of Sukarno. The reverse tick-tacking also came into play, and between them Critchley and Shann (and Tange) prevented a very serious Indonesian confrontation with Malaysia (and Singapore) from becoming much worse.

Remarkably, while all this diplomatic effort was being undertaken, Australia had an infantry battalion, the Fourth Battalion of the Royal Australian Regiment, stationed in the jungle near Bau on the Malaysian-Indonesian border, with the express order to repel Indonesian incursions. Holt and his party visited this battalion, which was commanded by Korean War veteran and Military Cross winner Lieutenant-

Colonel David Thomson. Nine years later Thomson became National Party MP for the North Queensland seat of Leichhardt and subsequently a minister in the Fraser Government. He took Holt on an inspection tour of the area by helicopter, along the often-unidentifiable border, and occasionally across it, where Indonesian forces were believed to be gathering. Holt said that night in Kuching: 'We'd better not go into details about this. The Indonesians may be a bit sensitive'. His little adventure was not reported.

While the confrontation with Indonesia in Borneo was important for Harold Holt on that 1966 trip, Vietnam was the highlight.

There he was feted by the US military commander, General William Westmoreland, and the South Vietnamese Prime Minister, the revolver-carrying Air Vice Marshal Nguyen Ky. On arrival at Saigon's Ton San Nut airport in his Viscount, he was given the VIP treatment, complete with bands, artillery salutes and red carpet, which stretched for 100 metres across the tarmac. His visit was timed to coincide with Anzac Day and he put on a truly memorable performance. Nobody in attendance doubted his sincerity, his political savvy, his showmanship and his bravery, when deliberately conspicuous as a potential sniper target in sparkling white safari suit, he stood on a dais at Bien Hoa airport and addressed the First Battalion, Royal Australian Regiment—while in the background Viet Cong mortar bombs were exploding along the heavily guarded perimeter.

Two days later, when he was having a beer with some Diggers at the Vung Tau rest base, he was at his affable and egalitarian best when, asked about his Anzac Day effort by one of them, he replied with feeling: 'Well, I'm sure glad the shit didn't hit the fan'. This from the most urbane man ever to sit in the prime minister's chair!

The accompanying Australian press party also was

grateful nothing untoward had happened, but did not learn until 25 years later how close a serious mishap had been. The journalists were in a US Chinook helicopter which landed them on a grassy verge at Bien Hoa airport, but the doors were not opened for some minutes. When the media representatives eventually were allowed to alight, two Australian officers were waiting. Sternly, they said something to this effect: 'Keep close together and please just all follow us closely this way, around to the other side of the chopper, for a picture.' There, a group photograph was taken. On 26 April 1991, former Army public relations officer Captain (and prominent Brisbane journalist) Ken Blanch, who had been one of those Australian officers, revealed that 25 years earlier, the Chinook had put us down in a minefield. While the photograph was being taken, other Australian soldiers worked out an exit path.

However, if the Prime Minister and his press party escaped personal injury at Bien Hoa as the Vietnam issue hotted up, the Opposition Leader, at home, did not. Sadly, Australia witnessed a political assassination attempt. On 21 June 1966, Arthur Calwell was the main speaker at a rowdy anti-Vietnam rally of about 400 people at the Mosman Town Hall in Sydney, and made his opposition to conscription his topic. After the meeting he was settling himself in the front passenger seat of his Commonwealth car, when Peter Raymond Kocan, aged 19, came running towards him.

As Calwell said later: 'I thought he might be just another well-wisher... so I started to wind down the car window to shake hands with him.' Fortunately, Calwell did not get that far, because Kocan produced a sawn-off shotgun from under his long coat and fired point blank. The thick glass window shattered and Calwell, luckily with his spectacles on, felt a 'stinging sensation' as glass particles peppered his jaw.

Calwell was shocked but not seriously hurt, but if the window had been open he almost certainly would have been killed. Kocan was charged and committed to a mental hospital. A concerned Holt said in Canberra that Australian public life up to then had been 'singularly free of episodes of violence' and that he deeply deplored the 'violation of our democratic traditions'.

A few weeks later, in an incident which Holt and police asked the few journalists who knew not to report for security reasons, a lone sniper fired a single rifle shot at him from a tree near Parliament House, as he worked in his corner office at night, lights ablaze and curtains open. The bullet cracked a window, Holt was not hurt, and according to police the sniper was caught and charged with a different offence, and there was virtually no publicity. But as a result of these two incidents, one highly publicised and affecting the Opposition Leader and the other under-publicised and affecting the Prime Minister, Australia would never be the same again.

Whereas up to then there had been sanguine security arrangements for political figures—prime ministers, ministers and opposition leaders could be approached by just about anybody at any time in public—serious protective measures were quickly put in place and have been tightened ever since. The inevitable effect has been to make political leaders more remote from their constituents, using radio and television and newspapers to communicate but increasingly eschewing personal contact.

Sometimes security has been carried to extremes. One of the most hilarious incidents seen by the author was the sight of Doug Anthony, 10 years later as acting Prime Minister in Malcolm Fraser's absence, being followed to the Canberra rubbish tip one Saturday afternoon by a police security car while he disposed of his household garbage from a utility.

As 1966 progressed, Holt continued to push his pro-Vietnam policy, but the war was escalating to a horrendous stage that neither he nor Menzies nor US President Lyndon Baines Johnson had envisaged. Backed by McEwen, Holt remained convinced that Australia's participation was correct, on the grounds it was in Australia's national interest that the USA remain committed militarily in Asia.

President Johnson makes no secret of why he is visiting Australia —nor does Holt. (This cartoon was inspired by a famous photograph by David Moore)

It was against that background that Holt made his subsequently much-criticised 'all the way with LBJ' statement to Johnson at the White House. In Washington it was clear to Holt and his party that opposition to Johnson's course was growing in the Congress as US casualties mounted and television brought the war into American homes.

Johnson needed to demonstrate he had allies in Vietnam, token though their efforts were in comparison with the logistical might of the US military machine. Holt needed to be reassured that the US alliance with Australia was rock-solid. As they sweated in that northern summer, each bolstered the other, but his 'all-the-way' rhetoric was to haunt him to his watery grave.

For his part, Johnson repaid the political debt in full. Knowing there was an election due for the House of Representatives by the end of 1966, he accepted Holt's invitation to make a visit to Australia—the first by a US president—and he carried it out with presidential panache, with an entourage that exceeded any of Queen Elizabeth's, and in robust Tammany Hall style, without any inhibitions about the purpose.

Australians accustomed to precise timetables and formal visits by the British Royals, which were the only benchmarks they knew for such events, were staggered as the tall swashbuckling Texan made his informal progress in his Boeing 707 Air Force One jet, first to Canberra, then to Sydney and Brisbane. He was always behind schedule, always stopping to plunge into crowds to shake hands and kiss babies, always handing out special LBJ ballpoint pens, always stressing the importance of Vietnam and the value he placed on Australia's support. And he was always accompanied by a veritable army of secret service guards in cars and on foot, headed by a personal bodyguard who revelled in the name of Rufus Youngblood.

Johnson even laughed good-humouredly at the buxom young protesters outside his Canberra base, the Canberra Rex Hotel, who bounced around in T-shirts bearing the slogan: 'Make love, not war.' In Brisbane, he made a point of staying in the same room, in Lennons Hotel, that World War II hero General Douglas MacArthur had used.

For Holt domestically it worked a treat. In one speech, Johnson flamboyantly said: 'The world needs Australia at this critical hour—all the way.' In Sydney, Liberal Premier

Robin Askin got so carried away with enthusiasm that when growing bands of protesters tried to stop Johnson's progress by throwing paint over the presidential car and lying down in front of it, he shouted: 'Run over the bastards.'

Holt went to the polls a few weeks later. He fought the election on the issue of Vietnam and the US alliance, declaring: 'Australia must have strong and reliable friends. That is why we played our part in the making of the SEATO and ANZUS treaties, which carry with them responsibilities as well as benefits. Because of these responsibilities, Australian soldiers are fighting in Vietnam... the Communists will learn that free Asia, and friends of free Asia, will not lose heart.'

The outcome was never in doubt. The meetings were rowdy. People were arrested. The protests led by Left-wing Labor frontbencher Dr Jim Cairns increased. The Labor leadership was in tatters because of intense rivalry (and differing policy statements) between Calwell and Whitlam. Calwell shadow-boxed and knew Labor was beaten. So did Whitlam. The Holt-McEwen Coalition Government had a sweeping victory. Not unreasonably, Holt took the win as a mandate to pursue his Vietnam policy, and he started to increase Australia's troops commitment soon after.

From that high point in his political fortunes, however, Holt ran into trouble, and there were four main contributing factors in his decline through 1967: the *HMAS Voyager* aftermath; an RAAF VIP 'affair'; the politics of two by-elections, a half-Senate election and Gough Whitlam; and Vietnam.

The *Voyager* hangover came down hard and suddenly upon the head of Holt, and it was entirely his own fault. It happened on the night of 16 May 1967 in the House of Representatives. The catalyst was the new Liberal MP for the blue-ribbon Sydney seat of Warringah, barrister Edward St John, QC, who was intent on making his evangelistic independent mark. It was his maiden speech and he chose the *Voyager* disaster as his topic, and in particular the character of the *Voyager's* captain, Captain Duncan Stevens, who died in the collision.

Several Liberal MPs had been pressing for a fresh inquiry and a former Navy officer, Peter Cabban, who had served with Stevens, recently had alleged that Stevens had been a serious drinker. St John, with the court-room manner of barrister addressing a jury, took it from there, with an increasingly angry Holt sitting at the centre table.

'Is it irrelevant,' asked St John, 'that the captain of the destroyer when in port was perpetually drunk? Or have I lost the meaning of the word "irrelevant"?' Holt, furious that the *Voyager* controversy, which he had been trying to shut down, was being opened up again in this manner by one of his own backbenchers, swivelled in his chair and interjected: 'And what is the meaning of the word "evidence"?' He realised immediately what he had done. He, with a greater knowledge of parliamentary rules and procedures than anybody in the chamber, had committed the cardinal parliamentary sin of breaching the convention that maiden speeches are heard in silence. He had also publicly undermined his own Liberal fellow traveller.

His ministerial colleagues and backbenchers also knew he had blundered. In the pin-dropping silence that followed, St John paused and said quietly: 'I didn't expect to be interrupted by the Prime Minister.' A red-faced Holt slumped in his chair. It was the first public sign that he was feeling the pressures of his high office. Three days later he announced the appointment of a second Royal Commission into the *Voyager* disaster.

The RAAF VIP affair was, in isolation, an equally small event. It was totally unnecessary and did Holt just as much political damage when he failed to contain it. It arose out of a flight Menzies had approved in 1965 for Calwell to attend an ALP federal executive meeting in Perth. Calwell broke convention by taking two Labor Party officials with him on the RAAF aircraft, federal secretary Cyril Wyndham and Victorian secretary Bill Hartley. Twelve months later, Labor veteran Fred Daly decided to target Calwell, with whom he had fallen out, by asking Holt about the use and costs of VIP flights. But the casualty of Daly's aim turned out to be Holt, who accepted an explanation from his own department that passengers' names and flight details were not kept for long and so the answers to Daly's question were not available.

In 1967 other questions were asked, by several Senators, about other VIP flights and in reply the Air Minister, Peter Howson, repeated the strange 'no-answers' explanation devised by the Prime Minister's Department for Holt. However, an upset Air Department knew this was wrong and several senior RAAF officers contacted the Government Leader in the Senate, John Gorton, who knew from his wartime experiences as a fighter pilot that records were retained. Without consulting Holt, Gorton called for the records to be produced by the Air Force and tabled three flight authorisation books and 13 passenger manifests. The affair subsided in a sea of embarrassment for Holt, and for the second time his Liberal colleagues wondered about his ability to control his government. The effect was cumulative.

Meanwhile, striding confidently onto centre stage was Gough Whitlam, who had succeeded Calwell as Labor leader after the 1966 election, and he was looking for electoral contests. They came in the second half of 1967. The first was a by-election in Corio, centred on Geelong, and was caused by the retirement of former world champion bicycle rider and former Liberal Minister, Hubert Opperman. He had held the seat for 17 years and the Liberals were confident they could retain it. It was the first head-to-head test at the ballot boxes between Holt and Whitlam. Holt ignored local issues and campaigned on what he assumed was his tried-and-true formula of Vietnam and the US alliance. Whitlam campaigned on parochial issues such as suburban sewerage with the line: 'This is the most effluent nation on earth.' The result: Corio was captured for Labor with an absolute majority by Gordon Scholes, who went on to become one of Parliament's best Speakers.

The second contest was a by-election in the central Queensland seat of Capricornia, centred on Rockhampton and Gladstone. It was caused by the death of Labor MP George Gray, who had retained the seat only narrowly in the 1966 general election. The Queensland Liberals were confident they could win this one and so persuaded Holt. He saw Capricornia as a chance to redeem himself as a campaigner in the eyes of his followers, and he was not going to repeat his tactical Corio mistake. The Liberal candidate was a high-profile local figure who was strong on regional development. The Labor candidate was a Left-wing atheist and humanist doctor, Doug Everingham, whose endorsement Whitlam had personally and unsuccessfully opposed.

Holt put his heart and soul into the campaign. He campaigned strenuously on regional issues and went on pub-crawls with Zara. Whitlam kept some distance between himself and Everingham and also stuck to local issues. The Liberals thought they were home. They had overlooked the local general practitioner factor, the fact that Everingham was a well-known, caring and popular doctor. The result: the vote for Labor increased and it held Capricornia safely.

On top of these two by-elections came the half-Senate election in November. The results were inconclusive in terms of numbers of seats won and lost. By its very nature, the election could not change the government. But it was an Australia-wide event and there was a 5 per cent increase in support for Labor compared to the 1966 election and an 8 per cent drop for the Liberal and Country Parties. For the third time in four months, Holt's credentials as a vote winner were being questioned within his own ranks. The psychological damage was growing. Overriding all else remained the Vietnam War. As in the USA, the national mood was changing against what was increasingly perceived to be an unwinnable conflict. Holt had raised the Australian troops commitment, including the birthday-ballot conscripts, three times—in March 1966, December 1966 and October 1967—until it reached more than 8000.

Still Johnson, with his own domestic pressure against the war growing, was asking Holt for more Australians. Casualties were increasing. Holt knew it could not go on. Australia's limited defence resources were stretched to capacity. Finally the Services Chiefs of Staff committee asked the Cabinet to call halt and Holt agreed.

There were at least two occasions where Holt's own mood change and doubts about Vietnam were revealed. The first came during a late-night return flight to Canberra during the Senate election campaign on Holt's RAAF aircraft. As was his wont, he liked to yarn with Press Gallery journalists and even bat ideas around. When Vietnam came up, he said wearily: 'You know, I still think I'm right, but these casualties our boys are suffering are terrible, for everybody. I believe I know how John Curtin felt during World War II.'

The second occasion was truly remarkable. About a week later, I was in Whitlam's office, discussing the election campaign with him. His phone rang. It was Holt. This in itself was not surprising, since there are many personal friendships across the political divide. Whitlam regarded Holt as a likeable, decent and civilised man, and Holt reciprocated and liked Whitlam's repartee. What was unusual was the next bit.

There was some typical Whitlamesque banter, and then he stopped suddenly and said quietly and seriously: 'Harold, you know I will never do or say anything to hurt you personally.' Whitlam then put his hand over the telephone, turned to me and asked me to leave the room briefly, saying: 'Harold obviously has something on his mind and this had better be private.'

About 15 minutes later he called me back in and said: 'Well, obviously I can't tell you what that was about, but he really unburdened himself about Vietnam.'

'Why you', I asked Whitlam. 'Why me?', Whitlam replied. 'Well, I like Harold. We get on quite well on many things. I'm a bit worried about him.'

I believe that very private conversation with Holt, and presumably others he had, led Whitlam to suggest years later that Holt might have been so depressed towards the end of 1967 that he had become suicidal. Other people who knew Holt have speculated along similar lines.

I do not agree with that contention, for Holt's second and final year in office had not been totally disastrous, despite all the pressures mentioned.

In May, Holt's Government, with Whitlam in complete agreement and even urging him on, had put two proposals to the people to amend the Constitution by referendum. One was to break the nexus between the two chambers of federal Parliament, which provides that the House of Representatives must be as nearly as practicable twice the size of the Senate, and so prevents the former being enlarged to allow for increased population without causing an unnecessary increase in the latter. This proposal, like all but eight put in referendums since Federation, was defeated overwhelmingly.

But the second proposal, seeking to give the

Commonwealth responsibility for Aboriginals, was carried overwhelmingly. Holt, a conservative in many ways, had shown genuine small-l liberal colours when it came to Aboriginals, just as he had done when he eased immigration laws to stop discrimination against non-Europeans. The tragedy is that the promise engendered for indigenous people in that 1967-referendum proposal put by Holt is still to be fulfilled.

The second notable win for Holt came only a few days before he drowned, and was over that doughtiest of politicians, John McEwen. McEwen wielded huge power and influence as Country Party leader, deputy Prime Minister, and Trade and Industry Minister, and was a proponent of all-round protection for secondary and primary industries alike with a system of tariffs and subsidies.

On 18 November, Britain devalued sterling by 14 per cent, and with McEwen overseas on a trade trip, the Holt Cabinet, on the advice of the Treasury, decided not to follow suit. A furious McEwen launched into savage criticism of Treasurer William McMahon and on return to Australia in December, issued a statement, which in effect challenged the authority of Holt. McEwen said: 'It is sad and serious that the decision (not to devalue) strikes in a most selective manner at our wealth-producing industries, both primary and secondary.'

Holt on this occasion stood up to McEwen. He publicly rejected McEwen's stand immediately and questioned McEwen's adherence to the principle of Cabinet solidarity in the process. McEwen knew he had gone too far. He backed off.

On the evening of Friday, 15 December 1967, Holt had Christmas drinks at The Lodge for members of the Press Gallery. He was in a joyful mood and he was celebrating. As a few journalists left in a group, he said to us: 'I'm going to

Melbourne for the weekend, but I'll see you all back here on Monday and I'll give you the detailed background to my little to-do with Jack. It's a good story for you.'

It was not to be. At 11.15 on Sunday morning, 17 December, Harold Holt walked alone into a raging sea off Cheviot Beach at Portsea on the Mornington Peninsula, and disappeared. His body was never found. But whatever was his state of mind, I do not believe it was suicidal. Rather it may well have been elation, and confidence that if he could beat McEwen, he could conquer the cruel sea. And having done that he had every intention of returning to Canberra to reveal the details of how he had got the better of 'Black Jack' McEwen!

At the memorial service for Holt at St Paul's Cathedral in Melbourne, there assembled the greatest international congregation Australia has ever seen. It included Prince Charles as representative of Queen Elizabeth; the man Holt had beaten for the deputy Liberal leadership, Governor-General Lord Casey; four presidents (Johnson, Marcos of the Philippines, Park of South Korea and Thieu of South Vietnam); five Prime Ministers (McEwen of Australia, Wilson of Britain, Kittikachorn of Thailand, Holyoake of New Zealand, and Lee Kuan Yew of Singapore); and three former Prime Ministers (Menzies, Arthur Fadden and Labor's Frank Forde).

To this very formal end of the Holt era, the issue of Vietnam overshadowed all else. Johnson used the memorial service as an occasion for a summit meeting of the Vietnam allies and he was surrounded by police and security guards—led by his ever-present personal bodyguards, Rufus Youngblood and Clint Hill, who slipped into the pew immediately behind him.

Dozens of other security men mingled in the congregation. The most incongruous of all in that place of peace were Johnson's special guards, with sub-machine pistols and facing the audience, who patrolled behind the altar and the organ as the service began... 'I am the resurrection and the life, saith the Lord.'

There have been a few singularly catalystic days in Australian politics, and 17 December 1967, when Holt drowned, was one of them. This was a day when the nature and character of Australian politics changed forever.

McEwen

GUNBOAT DIPLOMAT

**John McEwen, Country Party (1967–68)
23 days.**

'A supremely political animal, half lion, half fox.'
Graham Freudenberg, in A Certain Grandeur

'I do not trust you, Bill.'
John McEwen to William McMahon

John McEwen was on his soldier-settler farm at Stanhope in Victoria on that fateful December Sunday, when the telephone rang to tell him Harold Holt was missing. His informant was Lady Ansett, wife of transport magnate and close friend Sir Reginald Ansett, who had heard the news on a radio newsflash. McEwen had just put down the phone when it rang again and a staffer advised him officially.

Within the hour he was on his way—not to the centre of the prime ministerial drama at Portsea on Victoria's Mornington Peninsula, as might have been expected—but to the epicentre of the national political stage in Canberra.

Seldom, if ever, has an Australian political leader moved so quickly, so instinctively or so decisively at a time of such heightened drama and emotion. His instructions went out for an RAAF VIP aircraft to pick him up at Mangalore, and to his deputy leader of the Country Party, Doug Anthony, and the acting Secretary of the Prime Minister's Department, Peter Lawler, to meet him in Canberra. By mid-afternoon he was there. He made it clear to both that he was assuming command, and this became official following a meeting he had that evening at Government House with Governor-General Casey.

It was there that as deputy Prime Minister McEwen advised his old ministerial colleague Casey to appoint him Prime Minister until the Liberal Party had chosen Holt's successor, and it was there that Casey, well aware of the personal and policy rifts between McEwen and McMahon, accepted McEwen's advice. It was there that McEwen told Casey he would not serve in Coalition under McMahon.

On the same day McEwen took a further step to shut out McMahon. He started to stir the two most likely contenders for the Liberal leadership after McMahon: Paul Hasluck, who he would have preferred, and John Gorton. Both, along with External Affairs Department Secretary Sir

JOHN McEWEN

James Plimsoll, happened to be invited to a 'family supper' at the residence of the New Zealand High Commissioner in Canberra's dress circle road, 21 Mugga Way (which happened to be next door to the one provided for me by *The Courier-Mail*). Hasluck was phoned by McEwen just as he was leaving, at about 7.20 pm.

McEwen was frank with him, said he was just departing for Government House, and told Hasluck he would tell Casey it was 'more than doubtful' the Coalition would survive under McMahon. Hasluck thanked him and told McEwen that, as he knew, he also would find it impossible to work with McMahon as prime minister. Hasluck had already phoned his wife in Perth and told her the same thing, saying he would have to resign from the ministry if McMahon took over because, as she knew, he did not trust or respect McMahon. He thus shared McEwen's position on vetoing McMahon.

Inevitably, as at every other dinner table in the nation that night, the main conversation at the New Zealand High Commissioner's little dinner party was about Holt's disappearance, and at one point when they were alone, Hasluck suggested to Gorton that he consider making a bid for the Liberal leadership.

Hasluck told Gorton, then Education Minister and a Senator (and thus in the wrong Chamber to be Prime Minister) that in the House of Representatives there was nobody but himself. As Gorton was to put it later, Hasluck said to him: 'Look, Harold's gone and that means either you or I take over as PM. I think I am too old to do it so you will have to.' Gorton gave Hasluck no clear response. Later that night, soon after he got back to his Narrabundah home, Doug Anthony called, deputising for McEwen. The next morning Gorton phoned Hasluck to say he had decided to stand for the leadership. An initially unenthusiastic Hasluck himself was pressed by colleagues who included Gordon Freeth and Robert Cotton, and by Menzies in retirement, to seek the Liberal leadership also.

Gorton defeated Hasluck narrowly in the final party room ballot, understood to be by three votes. Both McEwen and Casey erred as a matter of principle (though not as a matter of pragmatic political judgement). In my view Casey should have called on McMahon, as deputy leader of the majority party, the Liberals, in the Coalition, to form a government until the Liberals voted on a new leader. But between them, McEwen and Casey sealed McMahon's fate. This was vintage McEwen, leader of the minority party in the Coalition, in his dour maturity and in most ruthless and determined mode, acting strategically and tactically. This was the ultimate example of how he could make the Country Party tail wag the Liberal dog.

Even McEwen of course had not always been mature. In 1939, at the age of 39, he had been in Federal Parliament for five years when the first leader of the Country Party, Earle Page, had set a precedent for his blackballing of McMahon. McEwen had been more impressionable when in the wake of the death of the (pre-Liberal) United Australia Party (UAP) Prime Minister Joe Lyons, Page had been commissioned by the Governor-General to form a government pending the election by the UAP of a new leader. Page, in a move that paralleled McEwen's in 1967, said he would not serve in any Cabinet that Robert Menzies might lead, and the Country Party formally declared it was 'definitely unable to cooperate with the Hon RG Menzies as its prime minister.'

However, the UAP elected Menzies as its leader despite Page's veto, and some Country Party MPs, notably a group of Queenslanders led by Arthur Fadden, then dissociated themselves from Page's move. In effect, the UAP had called

Page's bluff. But 28 years later, the Liberals were not about to do the same with McEwen. He was of sterner stuff.

First he spoke to Country Party colleagues, and particularly Doug Anthony, Ian Sinclair and Queenslander 'Ceb' Barnes, and ensured there would be no dissent within his own party. Then at background briefings (a procedure at which he was an exponent of the art of persuasion, even manipulation) McEwen let it be known he had conferred with Gorton and Hasluck and another senior Liberal, Allen Fairhall, and had told them the Country Party would not serve under McMahon. Then he called McMahon in and told him, and as he related later in notes for the national archives, when the gob-smacked McMahon asked why, he simply replied: 'My reason is that I do not trust you, Bill.'

At a quite dramatic press conference following his formal appointment as Prime Minister by Casey, McEwen was asked if he would say publicly that he would not accept McMahon as Prime Minister. He replied: 'Yes, I say to you I have told Mr McMahon that neither I nor my Country Party colleagues would be prepared to serve under him as prime minister. Mr McMahon knows the reasons. My senior Liberal Party colleagues not only know the reasons but knew the reasons before Mr Holt's death.'

Asked by Alan Reid if he would disclose the reasons, he said he would not. McEwen said he had 'decided firmly in my mind that what I have done is the correct course; that is, not allow the Liberals to go to an election (of their leader) ignorant of the attitude of myself and my Country Party colleagues.'

McEwen then put on his statesman's hat and said that in the atmosphere of mourning for Holt and with the impending visit of President Johnson and other 'great personages' for Holt's memorial service there would be no more domestic quarrelling and he would answer no further questions on the subject. 'Black Jack' McEwen had won the day. He may have been Prime Minister for only 23 days, from 19 December 1967 to 10 January 1968, but McEwen's influence on Australia and its affairs of state ranged far beyond that brief term. And indeed, that is not the shortest period. That honour goes to Labor's deputy leader Frank Forde, who was PM for only eight days after John Curtin died in 1945, before the ALP chose Ben Chifley.

Strange as it may seem, given his habit of pushing to the brink an issue in which he passionately believed, McEwen was, first and foremost, a coalitionist in what he regarded as equal partnership with three Liberal Prime Ministers: Menzies, Holt and Gorton. He was acting Prime Minister during their absences overseas or on holidays for a total of 550 days. His essential pragmatic policy was to stay in office. He knew exactly how far he could go.

Thus with the urbane Menzies he had the greatest rapport and enjoyed the greatest mutual respect. Though Arthur Fadden was Country Party leader and deputy Prime Minister from 1949 to 1958 (positions which McEwen believed should have been his years earlier and would have been but for the vagaries of party room voting), McEwen was always the dominant force in the party and beyond. Though Fadden was an efficient Treasurer and an affable foil to Menzies, it was McEwen who set the Coalition Government's economic policy with his controversial all-round protectionism for both the rural and manufacturing industries.

Menzies accepted this. Indeed there was virtually no dissension with 'McEwenism' in the early 1960s from any quarter of the Parliament, or the nation. For McEwen there was no such thing as a global level playing field. For him it was a case of not selling off any more of the Australian farm and of trying to buy back what had already slipped into the hands of foreign investors.

JOHN McEWEN

'Black Jack' McEwen makes his point with McMahon.

For McEwen, who had seen depression and wars and the nation in danger of being isolated, there was a need for Australia to manufacture whatever it possibly could, from aircraft to trains to ships. For McEwen there was always one economic policy: jobs and growth. For him there was the simple philosophy that Australia should sell wherever it could, whatever it could, especially its primary commodities and minerals, for the best prices it could get. Thus McEwen had no qualms about selling wool and wheat to Communist China when Australia refused to recognise it diplomatically.

His policies and profound influence have been decried by the free-market rationalists with hindsight in the moves towards globalisation in the 1980s and 1990s. It became conventional wisdom to rubbish him. But maybe the jury should still be out. Maybe he was right then but would be wrong now.

Inevitably it was in the Menzies years that McEwen was at his consistent strongest. He was advised and backed by one of Australia's greatest public servants, Sir John Crawford, as Secretary of the Trade Department, and the principal result of this combination—the favoured-nation Australia-Japan Trade Agreement—is rightly regarded as one of the Coalition Government's greatest achievements in the post-World War II era. Crawford was the nuts-and-bolts negotiating architect and McEwen was the one who persuaded Menzies and the Cabinet, at a time when anti-Japanese feelings still ran very high in the Australian community generally.

McEwen was quite sure, publicly, of his own strengths. There was no false modesty, no dissembling. But in private he suffered from dreadful nervous dermatitis, which got worse at times of increased pressure. On one occasion during the 1966 election campaign, he was in Maryborough, sitting on the veranda of an old Queenslander hotel, shoes and socks off, trousers rolled up, shirt open to the waist. His arms, legs and chest were red-raw. He was in agony and it was agonising to see him in such a state. The phone rang. It was the local radio station, seeking an interview. 'Just tell them, no,' he said, 'I can't think straight. Maybe it was the mud crabs we had for lunch at Childers.'

On the campaign trail McEwen could be a delight to cover, especially in the bush. He liked to travel in comfort and if the airfield runways were long enough he used one of the two RAAF VIP Viscounts, preferably the one that previously had been owned by the Union Carbide Company. If the runways could not handle the Viscount, he used one of the smaller and much slower RAAF 748s.

On one flight, from Brisbane to Emerald, he took a 748 and said on boarding: 'With a bit of luck this will take hours and there will be nobody to bother any of us.'

His simple and even simplistic message on the hustings in the bush was always on the same theme. Outlining the Coalition's record, he would say, in Maryborough, Bundaberg, Cairns, or wherever: 'First we made Australia safe, then we made it strong. You ask how did we do this? We made it safe by allying ourselves with the greatest military power on earth, the United States of America, through the ANZUS and SEATO treaties. We made Australia strong by negotiating important international trade treaties, and especially with Japan.'

'And who is it who did this?' he would call to his hall or street-corner audience, 'It is the Menzies-McEwen Government.' As the speech went on he would occasionally reverse this, so it became the 'McEwen-Menzies' Government (and later the 'Holt-McEwen/McEwen-Holt' and 'Gorton-McEwen/McEwen-Gorton' Governments).

He generally would end his speech with a variation of this theme: 'I am a simple farmer like yourselves. I understand your problems. In fact, I'm on my way back to my farm in Victoria now.' It was his firm rule never to dignify an opponent (Labor or Liberal) by mentioning his name.

As often as not during a campaign, McEwen would take his RAAF aircraft to Melbourne, grateful to get into the plane's air-conditioning and out of the Queensland summer heat and humidity which so aggravated the dermatitis he was desperately trying not to scratch. He would then head for a house he owned in upper-crust Toorak. He never told those anti-city, anti-southern Queensland farmers that he had such a fine abode as well as his farm.

His entourage was generally small—Press Secretary Bill Carew, a staffer from his Canberra office, one or two journalists, no security people or police—and all would often travel in the same car as him and invariably eat at the same table in an overnight stop at a motel. On one such occasion during the 1963 election, I asked him at dinner whether his switch to the 'McEwen-Menzies' description of the Government (the first time I had heard it) had been deliberate, he replied with a chuckle: 'What do you think? Bob knows what I'm up to. He also knows we have to keep winning in the bush.'

In line with this, McEwen made it clear that for him a Coalition win in the bush meant victory by the Country Party and not by the Liberals. In three-cornered contests he fought the Liberals implacably, often quite viciously. His desire to maintain the Country Party, and himself, as a formidable force, was intense and absolute.

He did, however, retract his Coalition leadership feelers in the first half of 1962 when Menzies belatedly took up Australia's running from him in Europe on the Common Market issue. He also retreated when Holt cried 'halt' to him in late 1967 after he criticised the Cabinet decision not to devalue the currency. But, in late 1962, he flatly opposed an electorate redistribution that threatened Country Party seats.

As he put it to a tense House, with Menzies listening, there would be no 'ifs' and no 'buts'. He took the Coalition marriage to the very edge of irrevocable divorce, and in that instance it was Menzies who decided not to test whether McEwen was bluffing. It was Menzies who backed off and dropped the whole idea, quaintly saying the debate was adjourned but would not be brought on again.

On another occasion McEwen exercised his power when the Liberal's Leslie Bury, in a speech to the Australian Institute of Management in Canberra, said that Australia's worry about the effect of Britain entering the European Common Market seemed far-fetched. Bury, who was Minister assisting the Treasurer, was an economist, a former Treasury adviser and a former executive director of the International Monetary Fund in Washington. His views therefore carried some weight. But they were anathema to McEwen, who publicly attacked Bury and asked Menzies to sack him. This Menzies promptly did, saying the convention of Cabinet solidarity had been broken.

It was never surprising that his Country Party followers revered McEwen. It was, however, always rather surprising to me that his personal staff, given the extraordinarily strenuous workload he placed on them, revered him to the extent they did. They were totally devoted to him. One of them, Mary Byrne, became his second wife (to the chagrin of another staffer) a year after his chronically-ill first wife, Dame Annie, died in 1967.

McEwen, unlike Menzies, was deliberate, calculating and foresighted when it came to establishing future party leaders. In the Liberal Party's case, it was clear that Holt, and nobody else, was Menzies' heir-apparent as Menzies' reign neared its end, but after Holt drowned suddenly the Liberal Party began to unravel. In the Country (later National) Party's case, however, McEwen carefully lined up three much younger colleagues, any one of whom could have succeeded him as leader: Doug Anthony, Ian Sinclair, and Peter Nixon. All three were in Parliament by 1963, and they were joined, at McEwen's urging, by a fourth potential party leader, Ralph Hunt, in a 1969 by-election.

When Hunt made a strong stump-stirring speech on a Saturday morning in the main street of Gunnedah during the campaign, McEwen, unable to hide his glee, called out to all and sundry: 'There, what do you think of my boy now.' Having helped his 'boys' into the Parliament, McEwen then made sure, in his various post-election dealings with Menzies, that they quickly gained places in the Ministry: Anthony into the Interior portfolio in 1964; Sinclair into Social Services in 1965, plus assistant to Trade Minister in Trade in 1966; and Nixon into Primary Industry in 1967.

To place Nixon in the Ministry, McEwen carried out what he later described as one of his most unhappy tasks. He told his 70-year-old and loyal friend, veteran Queenslander Charles Adermann, that he would have to stand down from Primary Industry. Adermann declared publicly that he would not do so. McEwen took him into his office, just off King's Hall. Half an hour later they came out. McEwen's arm was around Adermann's shoulder. Both were red-eyed from weeping. Adermann resigned from the Ministry the next day and Nixon was promptly sworn in.

McEwen's clashes with McMahon were legendary, particularly when McMahon became deputy Liberal leader and Treasurer under Holt after the departure of Menzies. The personality differences were obvious. McEwen was a dour Victorian farmer who had started from nothing and come up the hard way in rural industry politics. He was shy in private and blunt in public. McMahon was a glib Sydney socialite living on inherited wealth.

The policy differences were also just as obvious. McMahon and the Treasury opposed various 'interventionist' initiatives by McEwen and the Trade Department. They clashed over foreign investment in Australian companies like Heinz and Campbell soups, which Treasury supported with an open-door policy and McEwen opposed because it was 'selling off the farm'. They clashed over McEwen's tariff protection measures. They clashed over McEwen's proposal to establish the Australian Industry Development Corporation, which was to provide finance for selected industries and which McMahon, backed by the private banks, successfully blocked while Holt was Prime Minister, but which McEwen got up when John Gorton took over. They clashed over the activities of a largely anonymous Basic Industries Group, which set out to undermine McEwen and the Country Party.

They clashed over McMahon's apparent blatant leaking of Cabinet discussions to journalists Max Newton, who McEwen believed worked for the Basic Industries Group, and Alan Reid of the Sydney *Daily Telegraph*. (McEwen was more subtle and sophisticated. He had 'background briefings' with selected journalists, including myself and Ian Fitchett of *The Sydney Morning Herald*, in which he would outline his own and what he would describe as basic government thinking, without getting into Cabinet details or personalities.)

McEwen and McMahon clashed to such an extent that Holt once had to force them to shake hands after a Cabinet meeting. On another occasion, Casey intervened as Governor-General, privately but unsuccessfully, to try to get 'his Ministers' to settle their differences.

Ironically, however it was not Bill McMahon who was to become McEwen's most tenacious and effective opponent against protectionism. It was a little-known Liberal backbencher from South Australia, a farmer, Charles Robert ('Bert') Kelly, whose father Stan had been a member of the Tariff Board. Kelly was a highly principled, highly likeable, highly amusing, and deliberately self-effacing and self-rumpled character. Kelly said later his sole purpose in standing for Parliament in 1958 was to oppose 'McEwenism' and promote the cause of free trade. Initially he seldom had an audience, either in Parliament or the media. Kelly used to joke that he held the record for emptying the Chamber of its MPs in the fastest time.

McEwen at first ignored him. But Kelly's persistent needling and questioning of McEwen on protectionism, in the House and in the joint parties room, gradually took effect. It finally got under McEwen's skin. Kelly became an even more significant advocate of free trade when *The Australian Financial Review* took him on as one of its longest-running columnists under the pseudonym of 'The Modest Member'.

McEwen never quite got used to handling Kelly and occasionally would simply sit silent and stony-faced on the frontbench and not even answer a Kelly question. This would force the Speaker, Sir William Aston, finally to call for the next question. On one occasion, McEwen's response to Kelly was to say: 'That question is not worthy of a reply.' But it was Kelly who, more than any other person in Australia, was the architect of the sea change in economic thinking from protectionism to free trade and market forces.

McEwen, like Menzies, retired from Parliament of his own volition, but, unlike Menzies, hung on just a fraction too long. He did so, however, because as he said in his memoirs for the archives, he felt Coalition stability had to be maintained and he was the one to do that.

He made no secret of the fact that he would have preferred Paul Hasluck to have become Prime Minister instead of John Gorton and he urged Hasluck to actively get a campaign going for the Liberal leadership in that emotional Christmas-New Year period of 1967-68. This was something Hasluck, who believed he could win the leadership on perceived merit and intellect alone, refused to do. Indeed, McEwen once told me he would have departed earlier if Hasluck had been prime minister.

McEwen certainly was a steadying influence in the Coalition Government led by Gorton, who he regarded, correctly, as a good knockabout larrikin bloke with good intentions but no self-discipline. He came to realise that Gorton was losing control of the Liberals. He became disenchanted with Gorton's growing disinclination to consult him or often Cabinet generally. McEwen became especially upset at the manner in which Gorton discarded Sir John Bunting as Secretary of the Prime Minister's Department and installed Sir Lenox Hewitt instead. He had

had seen Bunting as an important element of administrative continuity from the Menzies era. Hewitt and Gorton's young secretary Ainsley Gotto became Gorton's keepers and often made access to him very difficult.

There was one notable occasion when (as he related to me later, when reminiscing on the eve of his retirement) McEwen wanted to talk urgently with Gorton and went along the corridor to the Prime Minister's office. Hewitt was attending to some papers in the little anteroom. 'Is the Prime Minister in his office?', McEwen asked Gotto. She replied: 'He's busy.' Said McEwen: 'I need to see him. Is there anyone with him?' Again she replied: 'No, but he is busy. He is not able to see anyone.' At which point, McEwen, for so long a dominant Coalition partner, stormed: 'Out of my way, woman,' and burst in on a startled Gorton. 'John was quite surprised, I think', chortled McEwen as he related this, 'but I made my point fairly clearly'.

With the Liberals' increasing disarray and discontent with Gorton growing within the party ranks, McEwen became deeply concerned, even to the point where he accepted he could not veto McMahon forever. Hasluck had been appointed/removed/sidelined to Yarralumla as Governor-General by Gorton and the Liberals were running light on leadership talent.

After the 1969 election, in which the Liberals lost seats, Liberal frontbencher David Fairbairn stirred the pot on 3 November by announcing in Melbourne he would challenge Gorton for the leadership. He added that if McMahon stood for the leadership also and won, he (Fairbairn) would willingly serve under him.

McEwen was also in Melbourne, and when asked virtually immediately if he would again blackball McMahon, he would not be drawn. He simply said that if McMahon wanted to know his attitude, 'he will come and see me'. Bill McMahon, needing no further invitation and also in Melbourne, promptly phoned McEwen and arranged to see him that same afternoon at McEwen's Toorak house. He emerged bubbling with joy, literally bouncing, and said (pathetically for a putative Liberal leader, but the incident showed the clout McEwen still wielded): 'He'll have me. Jack will have me!'

McMahon later that day formally announced his decision to stand against Gorton, at what was to be the first of two attempts. He did not win at that Liberal Party meeting but Gorton's margin was slender. McEwen, rather more dignified and restrained than McMahon, issued a statement, which said he had told McMahon that if he was chosen as Liberal leader, 'I would not refuse to join him in a coalition, subject to having a satisfactory understanding with him on a variety of matters.'

Finally, ever the realist, as he felt the free-trade forces slowly massing, as the pressure took its toll on him physically, as his dermatitis got much worse, as Lady Mary McEwen increasingly suggested he call it a day, as he came to feel the Country Party succession was established, and as he saw the relentless ascendancy of Whitlam and the writing on the wall for the Coalition, he decided to retire. He announced his intention to do so 'in a few months', in November of 1970 as the parliamentary session came to an end.

It was then that he revealed what he regarded as his single greatest achievement. At a memorable lengthy get-together with Press Gallery members that night, a gathering at which he provided drinks and food and was prepared to yarn on-the-record for hours, McEwen was asked the obvious question: What had been the most significant thing he had done during his 37 years in federal Parliament?

His questioners assumed it would be the Australia-Japan trade Agreement, or maybe his ascendancy to the prime ministership in his own right, albeit briefly, in 1967 and his vetoing of McMahon. Not so. Neither of the above. What he immediately hailed as his 'greatest achievement' was a pure old-style colonial coup. An adventure of gunboat diplomacy (and well described in Peter Golding's *'Black Jack' McEwen, Political Gladiator*). McEwen claimed he master-minded a coup to stop the French territory of New Caledonia, only 1000km east of the Queensland coast, from falling into enemy hands in September of 1940, early in World War II.

At the time, McEwen was a 40-year-old External Affairs Minister in the first Menzies Government. France had just surrendered to Nazi Germany, the collaborationist Vichy Government suddenly was in control of the French colonies in the South Pacific, and McEwen was worried Japan would take over New Caledonia. Records show that though Japan was more than a year away from entering the war, a meeting of the Australian War Cabinet in June 1940 discussed the ramifications of a possible Japanese occupation of New Caledonia.

The services Chiefs of Staff advised against Australia attempting to take over the French territory because it did not have the military strength to defend New Caledonia against a Japanese invasion. The Australian Government dithered, and sought advice from the British Government, which at first recommended caution in any move on New Caledonia. But then the pro-German Vichy Government despatched a sloop, *Dumont d'Urville*, to Noumea to shore up its regime there.

McEwen apparently disagreed with Australia's caution and wanted action. He and the External Affairs Department Secretary, Colonel WR Hodgson, decided to organise a coup, though the Department's records do not state that McEwen was personally responsible. 'The matter was not discussed in Cabinet,' McEwen recalled on that November 1970 night. 'I put it up to Menzies. It was all done very quickly.' The two agreed there had to be 'aggressive diplomacy'. It was *Boys' Own Annual* stuff. McEwen then contacted a Mr Bertram Charles Ballard, a French-speaking solicitor living in the New Hebrides, and asked him to accept appointment as Australia's official representative in New Caledonia, to make contact with the anti-Vichy Free French people there and lay the foundations for a revolution.

At McEwen's request, Menzies then asked British Prime Minister Winston Churchill to arrange for the Free French resistance leader, Charles de Gaulle, to direct the French Resident Commissioner for the New Hebrides, one Henri Sautot, to lead a landing of Free French supporters, who had gathered from other French islands, on New Caledonia.

This was to be an expedition that Australia would organise. The Australian Government chartered a Norwegian freighter (so as not to alert the Vichy French) to take Sautot and his followers to New Caledonia. At the same time, McEwen directed the Australian cruiser HMAS *Adelaide* to stand off Noumea as Sautot arrived in the Norwegian ship. *Adelaide* then sat in the harbour at Noumea, guns trained on the smaller pro-Vichy sloop *Dumont d'Urville*, while Sautot disembarked.

The gunboat diplomacy worked. The local pro-Vichy administration surrendered and was later dropped off in French Indo-China near Saigon by the Norwegian freighter. An administration loyal to de Gaulle was installed in New Caledonia instead. The result was that when Japan entered the war in December 1941, New Caledonia was in Allied hands and not Axis hands. The Japanese never got a footing there and it became a major US base as the Pacific War developed. As McEwen put it, 'if the Japanese had established themselves on New Caledonia in 1940 before they were at war with us, the menacing outcome for Australia would not have borne thinking about.'

It was an enlightening evening, in more ways than one. Because I came away realising that throughout his career, McEwen, for all his cunning, had always been a gunboat diplomat, full-on and frontal when necessary, with little concern for finesse. Indeed I was prompted to remember that McEwen had laid down his credo precisely at a Country Party Federal Council meeting in Canberra in 1965. He said: 'Out of my long experience in political life, I would say that the man who is incapable of inspiring some fear in his political opponents doesn't amount to a row of beans when the chips are really down.' He was referring not just to the Labor Party, but to 'our allies, the Liberal Party.'

'The real skill in politics', he said, 'is to establish in the minds of your opponents that they had better be pretty fearful of what you might do to them, and on the basis of that get what you want without fighting.'

John McEwen formally resigned from Parliament on 1 February 1971. Having sold his farm, he retreated to his Toorak house with Lady McEwen. Like Menzies he did not look over the shoulders of his successors. He died in November 1980.

With his departure came the end of the long conservative Menzies-Holt-McEwen era. It had encompassed wars and danger and peace and prosperity, party in-fighting and significant Coalition unity as well as a Labor Party split. It had been an era noted for low unemployment and low inflation and low foreign debt. It had not been complicated by environmental, Aboriginal or feminist issues.

It left many legacies and ironically, two major and unintended ones.

First, the Vietnam War, in which Australia's

participation had been so staunchly advanced by Menzies, Holt and McEwen, spawned a whole new generation of bright, protesting people—for example, Gareth Evans, John Button and Neal Blewett—who revitalised the Australian Labor Party and provided its future muscle and impetus for the Whitlam and especially the Hawke and Keating administrations.

Second, McEwen's protectionism specifically spawned and lifted the profile of his chief opponent 'Bert' Kelly, champion of free trade and market forces. Kelly's disciples expanded out of forums such as the HR Nicholls Society and included influential Liberals such as John Hewson (who would become senior adviser to Treasurer John Howard and Opposition Leader), Peter Costello (who would become Treasurer) and Ian McLachlan (who would become National Farmers' Federation president and Defence Minister).

McEwen essentially set Australia's economic agenda for the best part of four decades. But his opponents and critics were the ones who did so for the last two decades of the 20th century and the start of the 21st. He would have been horrified at the high unemployment, shrinking manufacturing base and huge foreign debt. His nay-sayers believe his unshakeable convictions and refusal to change would have put him out of his depth in the new world of technology, e-commerce and globalisation.

Nevertheless, McEwen was a giant in his time, almost matching Menzies. It is fitting that when the National Party built its own headquarters in Canberra, about 100 metres from the Liberal Party headquarters named after Menzies, it named its building not after Earle Page, the Country Party founder, but after McEwen.

And so John McEwen House it is. Eventually history will show whether he was right and how long the party he led with such force will survive.

Gorton

LARRIKIN AT LARGE

John Grey Gorton, Liberal (1968–1971)
3 years, 2 months

'Gorton, whose feel for the nation was abiding, and whose first anxiety was to prosper its cause.'

Sir James Killen

'Australia has more to it than bloody boongs and pop-singers.'

Gorton, summing up Expo 70 in Japan

No person came to the office of Prime Minister of Australia supported by greater public goodwill, or in more unusual circumstances, than John Gorton in January of 1968.

No Prime Minister squandered immense popularity quite as quickly.

No Prime Minister was subject to such sustained attack, by both his official Labor Opposition and conservative Liberal and National Party detractors.

When he defeated Paul Hasluck for the Liberal leadership, resigned from the Senate, assumed the prime Ministership, aged 57, without being a Member of Parliament, and stood successfully in the by-election for the Melbourne seat of Higgins left vacant by the disappearance of Holt, it became clear he was a most likeable Australian larrikin, irreverent, casual and contemptuous of conservative convention. He also was the first Prime Minister to really understand he was in the new age of television, and how to use it to his advantage.

Of the four candidates in the leadership campaign (the others being Hasluck, Leslie Bury and Billy Snedden), he was the only one to use television widely and wisely. He realised the objective was to leave a favourable visual impression with viewers and thus the Liberal MPs who would cast their votes. Content and details concerned him little, then or later. It was the basic thrust that mattered.

Asked in one television interview what kind of a man and potential prime minister he was, he replied in delightful self-deprecatory manner: 'Six feet one inch tall, 12 stone in weight and passably good-looking.' It was a lightweight response. But it appeared to go over big on television.

Two days into the Higgins by-election campaign Gorton was running notoriously late for appointments and meetings. It took only those two days for the even more irreverent members of the Press Gallery to run a sweep, at $1 a head, on exactly how many minutes late he would be each time.

On one occasion, he was precisely 47 minutes late for a press conference he had called, and I was the winner, because I had picked 45 minutes and nobody expected him to be later than that! He was surprised when greeted with applause and not scowls as he entered, and laughed when told the reason. As he left the conference later, he stopped by me and said quietly, with his war-crumpled face twisted into trademark grin: 'How late do you want me to be tomorrow?' There was nothing disingenuous about Gorton. He loved it.

The reasons for Gorton's immense initial popularity were fourfold: first, there was huge public and even corporate relief—after the shock of Holt's drowning and the turmoil within the Coalition created by McEwen's veto of McMahon—that the Liberals had quite smoothly chosen a new leader; second, there was a honeymoon with the media; third, there was Gorton's quite interesting background, of which the people were only then becoming fully aware; and fourth, his was a fresh face projecting avowed Australian nationalism.

For Gorton, rightly, was perceived as the first modern nationalist. He was ahead of Gough Whitlam, of whom many people were not yet sure and who had not yet been tested at a general election as Labor leader.

Gorton was also capable of being cast, as he was by his press secretary the ubiquitous Tony Eggleton, as an educated battler-hero. The son of his Victorian orchardist father's mistress Alice Sinn, he had been educated at Geelong Grammar and Oxford. His battered face, so ugly it was handsome, was testimony to three crashes he had survived as an RAAF fighter-pilot in the South-West Pacific in World War II.

The wartime fighter pilot tries his dab hand at government.

If there are two words to best describe John Grey Gorton as Prime Minister, they are 'unconventional' and 'unpredictable'. Gorton's unorthodoxy was quick to surface. One of his first administrative acts was both unfortunate and unnecessary. When he shunted off Sir John Bunting, one of the long-serving public service mandarins of the Menzies era, from the position of Secretary of the Prime Minister's Department, he lost a rock of stability and constancy that the times needed.

Menzies, who had described Bunting as the 'prince of public servants', said nothing publicly but was known to be angry. Gorton was far from contrite. He was to later recall, in characteristic blunt fashion: 'Some public servants saw their role as being to give the Government advice and further, that their advice had to be taken. I didn't agree. We didn't take their advice very frequently. I got Len [Sir Lenox] Hewitt in as head of the Prime Minister's Department and hived Bunting off as Secretary of the Cabinet office, and we went ahead not taking much notice of Bunting. I don't think this did any serious harm.'

At the same time Gorton's appointment of the attractive and highly intelligent 21-year-old Ainsley Gotto as his private secretary raised conservative eyebrows, also unnecessarily. Appearances mattered, then as now, in the most powerful office in Australia.

Both Hewitt and Gotto were extremely efficient, hard-working, protective of, and loyal to, Gorton. So much so that just about everything and everybody channelled through them. Such protectiveness sustained him for a long time. But the corollary was isolation for Gorton and that eventually contributed to his undoing. When he dropped Liberal MP Dudley Erwin, once a core supporter of Gorton, from the Ministry, Erwin gave this assessment of the reason: 'It wiggles, it's shapely, it's cold-blooded, and its name is Ainsley Gotto.'

Twenty-four years later, Gorton himself referred to the innuendo involving Gotto: 'Yes, there was innuendo,' he said, 'but I mean... bloody hell, innuendo is not something that has been proved. It's just this whispering around the place... I was employing her. Why should you sack somebody who is efficient and doing the job well? Why should that person be in the position of being sacked because of innuendo?'

Gorton's forays into the foreign policy arena were typically unpredictable, the result of his tendency to make policy on the run, with little apparent consultation with Ministers, backbenchers or public service advisers. He followed his gut nationalistic instincts and often he was seen, in retrospect, to be correct. Yet as far as his orthodox, critical conservative colleagues were concerned, he was to become an object of dismay and a catalyst for dissension. For the accompanying reporter there was never a shortage of news items.

In May of 1968, for example, when the Vietnam War

was still regarded officially as winnable by the USA, and when Australia's commitment to it was still accepted as justifiable by most Australians, Gorton surprised his Cabinet, and McEwen and Defence Minister Allen Fairhall in particular, with a statement to a joint Liberal-Country Party meeting that the established concept of 'forward defence' might have to be abandoned.

Instead, he said, Australia might have to develop an 'Israeli-type defence scheme', under which elements in the civilian population would be trained in arms in readiness for an emergency. Instead of holding forward positions in South-East Asia, as Australia did in Vietnam, Papua New Guinea, Singapore and Malaysia, it might have to shift the emphasis to mobile forces that it could deploy in the area in alliance with others. Since forward defence was long-established Coalition policy, Gorton in one fell swoop managed to upset many Liberals, the Country Party, the USA, and the Rightist Democratic Labor Party, on whom the Coalition depended for preferences in any general election.

Gorton's timing also was awry, for two reasons: first because the leaders of Singapore (Lee Kuan Yew) and Malaysia (Tunku Abdul Rahman) had recently formally asked Australia to keep its forces after the proposed British military withdrawal East of Suez in 1971; and second, because Gorton's statement, despite much hosing down in the background by the Defence and External Affairs departments, was assumed by the US Embassy to be deliberate. It was just two weeks before he was due in Washington on his first official visit as Prime Minister, mainly to discuss Australia's defence ties, meaning its commitment to South-East Asia and the Vietnam War, with President Johnson.

Strangely, unlike his predecessors and his successors, Gorton went without any expert advisers from the Defence or External Affairs departments. His official entourage comprised only his American-born wife Bettina, Hewitt, Gotto, Eggleton and a man to handle travel arrangements.

Gorton made a muddle of it, mangling the English language and his thoughts in the process. At a press conference at Blair House in Washington, he was asked whether the ANZUS Treaty, cornerstone of the Australia-US alliance, applied to Australian forces in Malaysia and Singapore.

He replied: 'I don't know I can give you any definite answer to that. ANZUS is a treaty. I think it applies in certain defined areas. But I would want to check that with the External Affairs people before I was sure that was correct. But by and large, I think it has been, what shall I say? I cannot think of the exact words—a matter never spelled out whether it applied in the Malaysia or Singapore area or not... Well, you are asking really the sort of questions which one can pursue to the point where it is the whole sort of subject of discussions. And I do not think I am free to do that.'

It was little wonder the hawkish US Administration became increasingly concerned and even confused. A year later, in May of 1969, Gorton virtually echoed Harold Holt's 'All the way with LBJ' sentiments when he told Johnson at the White House: 'Sir, we will go Waltzing Matilda with you.' However this pledge was not as unconditional as some tabloid newspapers made out, because Gorton had added that it would be dependent on the South Vietnamese Government maintaining its authority and on the USA maintaining its commitment to the South-West Pacific.

Meanwhile, the tide was turning in Vietnam, and Gorton, again having followed his gut instincts, already knew it from first-hand observation. He had made a visit there in 1968 to see the Australian and New Zealand troops who were serving in a combined Anzac Battalion of the

Royal Australian Regiment, and to confer with the USA and South Vietnamese military and civilian strategists in Saigon. He was the first allied leader to visit Vietnam after the Tet offensive, and over drinks with a few of the accompanying Australian journalists in Kuala Lumpur the night after leaving Saigon, Gorton put his comments off-the-record. He said, very soberly and (surprising those present) very succinctly: 'You know, I still think our Vietnam policy was and is correct. But we're not going to win this one. We're going to have to cut our losses.'

I subsequently wrote a column headed: 'War, war everywhere and never a win in sight', which drew on Gorton's new pragmatic approach. Soon after he returned to Canberra he told Cabinet (and let this be known as background information) that no more Australian troops would be sent to Vietnam and he eventually took the decision to withdraw an Australian battalion.

The more's the pity, in retrospect, that often Gorton found himself unable to elucidate in public the way he could in private conversation. For at a press conference in Kuala Lumpur the day after his 'cut-our-losses' comment, when asked for his assessment of the Vietnam War which he had just left, he said, tiredly: 'It is apparent that fighting is continuing, and it is obvious that it is continuing. I will not go any more deeply into a military analysis than that.'

Asked a vague question about the 'general SEATO situation' (it being basically the SEATO treaty which the Menzies and Holt governments had invoked to cover Australia's participation in Vietnam), Gorton apparently misheard the question and replied: 'General Who?'

Gorton was in his swashbuckling prime during a visit to Papua New Guinea (PNG), then still an Australian colony, in July of 1970. Whitlam, deliberately stirring the pot, had preceded him a few months earlier as Opposition leader, urging early independence from Australia for the PNG people, and Gorton ran into inflamed and hostile audiences in Port Moresby and Rabaul in particular.

Rabaul was seething with unrest and thousands of Mataungan warriors, carrying spears, clubs and placards and in their ceremonial dress, turned out at the airport to air their grievances under the leadership of an impressive John Kaputin, later a prominent minister in the independent Papua New Guinea Government. They were hostile and certainly looked fierce. In the upshot, they were not violent but Gorton could not be certain of that beforehand. Some of his advisers suggested he give Rabaul a miss. Gorton would have none of that.

But he did agree that perhaps the RAAF aircraft carrying the Australian press should land first, virtually as a decoy, to see what the local reaction was to what the Mataungans might think was the prime ministerial plane. When the press plane was seen to be accepted his aircraft came in behind a few minutes later. Gorton was quite heavily and closely guarded by Australian security police and soldiers. As an extra precaution, fortunately unbeknown to the waiting massed Mataungans and most people in the Australian group, he carried a 25.20 pistol in his pocket as he made his speech about not holding up independence for a moment longer than when a majority of the people wanted it.

Some weeks later I heard about the pistol from one of his security men. I asked him about it one night when I saw him outside his office in Old Parliament House. He said: 'Well, I had my wife there, and I didn't want anything to happen to her.' He simply could not understand why he was even being questioned. Yet the thought of what might have been the mob outcome if such bravado had resulted in a pistol-packing Australian Prime Minister shooting at a

Mataungan on the Rabaul airstrip, remains horrifying more than three decades later.

At home, too, John Gorton showed, early in his reign, that he could be cavalier. During a tour of Western Australia in September 1968, he got word from the Treasury that a British firm was buying up shares in one of Australia's biggest insurance companies, MLC Limited. In that pre-globalisation era, there was much public concern at the increasing international ownership of Australian companies and resources. Gorton consulted only the ever-present Len Hewitt and reacted spontaneously.

High over the Nullarbor Plain en route back to Canberra at the end of an anti-clockwise trip around Australia, he announced to the accompanying press in his aircraft that because the MLC Company was registered in the Australian Capital Territory (ACT) the Commonwealth Government had the power to, and would, intervene and block any foreign takeover bid. He duly did so.

Obviously I, and other delighted journalists, filed this story to our newspapers as soon as we landed. Gorton was reflecting majority public sentiment. But he had gone against the advice of the Treasury and he had not consulted any Cabinet colleagues. He had not waited to confer even with the elder statesman of the Coalition, John McEwen (who, incidentally, would have agreed with him).

He had not consulted Establishment business leaders, as Menzies and Holt would have done. Though Gorton could justify his independent action and decisiveness, it was at that point that the establishment began to wonder about his style and the manner in which he might wield unpredictably his immense power-of-one in the future.

Though convention and due process seemed to be beyond him, there was never any doubt that Gorton had the personality and charm of a good bloke. I can attest to that personally. At the end of his 1968 visit, which took in Vietnam, Malaysia and Singapore, Gorton and his party had two days in Bali. This was for private 'rest and recuperation' on the way home (and Gorton managed to offend Indonesian Foreign Minister Adam Malik, who had flown specially from Jakarta, by virtually having nothing to do with him). Bettina Gorton, a scholar in Indonesian language and literature, had long been a close friend of artist Donald Friend, who lived and worked at that time in a hut-cum-studio nearby on the beach at Bali. One morning she said to me: 'I am going along the beach soon to see Donald. He wants me to take some of his pictures back to Australia to sell for him. Would you like to help me carry them?'

Needless to say, it was a marvellous experience seeing Donald Friend 'at home' and Bettina Gorton and I walked back along the beach to our hotel carrying about 20 of his paintings, rolled into cylinders and tied into bundles. About a week later, home in Canberra, she invited me to The Lodge one afternoon for an unrolling and viewing of the pictures. There was one, of a Bali beach scene, with which I was particularly enamoured and she said I could have first offer before she sold them all elsewhere for Donald Friend. The price, however, was several hundred dollars, and I had to turn her offer down.

The next day, I had a direct phone call from the Prime Minister in my office in Old Parliament House: 'Wally, it's John Gorton here. Betty tells me she has a painting you like but cannot afford. I'll lend you the money if you like.' With thanks and regret I turned his typically spontaneous offer down, saying there was no way a political correspondent in the Press Gallery could borrow money from a prime minister.

There was one other occasion when I had a particularly interesting phone call from Gorton, at about 11 pm at home. His brief message was this: 'I thought you'd like to know that some bastard's just climbed over the fence here at The Lodge and thrown some sort of acid in the swimming pool.' I started to ask for more details. 'That's it', he said, 'the bastard got away, this has not come from me, nothing more.' And he hung up. Naturally I phoned the story through to *The Courier-Mail*, embellishing it with the need for better security for public figures. The next day the report was at first vigorously denied by a Commonwealth Police spokesman, then the reaction changed to a 'no comment on security issues of any sort'. Then Gorton was asked if the report was correct. He also could have given the conventional 'no comment on security' response. He said laconically: 'I believe it is.'

None of which is to suggest that Gorton was all froth and fun and no substance—far from it. In the wake of the 1967 referendum, he was the first Prime Minister to appoint an Aboriginal Affairs Minister (Wentworth). He also backed McEwen's attempts to put Australian assets back in Australian hands and agreed to the formation of the Australian Industry Development Corporation.

He followed in Menzies' footsteps as a Cold War warrior. His Cabinet considered developing nuclear weapons for Australia and announced (but did not follow through) that a nuclear power plant would be developed at Jervis Bay. A vast nuclear power industry was on the drawing boards at one stage, with an amazing 26 reactors contemplated for construction in the 10 years from 1975 in New South Wales and Victoria alone.

Having implemented Menzies' education policies initially as Education Minister, he expanded on them as Prime Minister. He preserved the Great Barrier Reef from oil exploration which the Queensland Government wanted to allow. He gave significant Commonwealth backing to Australian art and film.

An avowed centralist, he clashed with conservative Premiers, especially Queensland's Sir Joh Bjelke-Petersen, when he sought to assert Commonwealth control with his Seas and Submerged Lands Bill, and pushed on regardless. One of Gorton's first acts was to deny the powerful veteran Victorian Premier Sir Henry Bolte access to a growth tax for his State. Bolte, who considered Gorton a lightweight, was incensed, and turned against him.

Nevertheless, though the Coalition's majority was substantially eroded by Labor under Whitlam in the 1969 election, Gorton remains the only Liberal leader since Holt not to have lost an election (discounting Alexander Downer, who in the 1990s was not leader long enough for an election to occur).

It is worth noting in passing that in October of 1969, Australia's economic growth rate was 6 per cent, its inflation rate 3 per cent, and unemployment less than 1 per cent.

John Gorton, however, was soon brought undone—by himself, by people who liked to think they were true-blue conservatives, by the acerbic evangelistic straight-laced Liberal MP Ted St John, by Whitlam, by Malcolm Fraser and by McMahon.

Gorton was never prepared to accept that the high office of Prime Minister carried with it the responsibility to stop living the casual, red-blooded Australian way he liked. But being seen as a 'good bloke' was not enough. He did realise the position put him under intense public (meaning media) scrutiny, but that did not concern him. Incapable of deviousness, he believed that to be open was to be successful and that little more was required.

Thus Gorton continued to invite Labor's Senate leader, Lionel Murphy, to have a friendly late-night drink in his office, just as he had done when he had been government leader in the less combative Upper House. This not only annoyed Opposition Leader Whitlam, but more importantly, it upset John McEwen, who was beginning to worry about Gorton's judgement.

Thus Gorton, when attending the World Expo 70 in Osaka on Australia's official day, decided spontaneous honesty rather than tact was the course to adopt. The main homespun Australian participants in the ceremony were a group of Aboriginals who performed traditional dances, Rolf Harris, and *The Seekers*. After the performance, the Australian officials responsible for coordinating Australia's contribution to Expo asked Gorton what he thought of it all as the prime ministerial party, including a few journalists, walked back to the Australian exhibition hall. Expecting to be complimented, the officials were as stunned as I was surprised when Gorton replied: 'Aah, Australia has more to it than bloody boongs and pop-singers.'

Thus Gorton, in October 1968, having been told by President Johnson that secret negotiations were under way with the North Vietnamese and that he hoped to announce cessation of the US bombing before the presidential election in November, promptly revealed this to three journalists in Parliament House at an impromptu gathering after a theatre party. The Johnson Administration vented its understandable rage to the Australian Embassy in Washington.

And thus about a week later, on 1 November 1968, Johnson formally announced the bombing halt, and Gorton happened to be guest of honour at the annual Press Gallery dinner, held at the old Park Royal Motel in Canberra. The US Ambassador, William Crook, invited him to call in at the US Embassy after the dinner to discuss details of Johnson's announcement and presumably to smooth over any diplomatic ill-feelings caused by Gorton's earlier indiscretion.

Despite several messages from the Embassy to Gorton at the dinner, asking at what time Ambassador Crook might expect him, Gorton lingered until about 1.30 am—and then took with him 19-year-old journalist Geraldine Willesee who, he said later, had asked him for a lift home. Fortunately the alert and ever-discreet non-drinking Tony Eggleton quickly followed Ms Willesee into the back seat of the prime ministerial car with the C1 number plate, which meant Gorton had to get into the front passenger seat.

For Gorton, the outcome was a fiasco. The news, rumours and innuendo first surfaced, not the next day in the mainstream media, as would now be expected, but several weeks later in the newsletter *Things I Hear* by Frank Browne. (Browne was one of the two journalists sent to jail by the Parliament in the Menzies era in the infamous privileges case of 1955.) It then was raised in the House first by NSW Labor MP Bert James, on 19 March 1969, and was taken up by Whitlam.

Gorton was partly saved by McEwen, who gagged further debate, only to find a self-righteously indignant St John attacking him from the Liberal backbench a few hours later, accusing him of prejudicing Australia's relationship with the USA. 'This was the Embassy of the United States, our most powerful ally,' thundered St John in his clinical courtroom manner, 'I cannot think that this is private life.' In the fuss both St John and Gorton got times wrong. St John said Gorton had left the Press Gallery dinner at 2.30 am and the US Embassy at 5.30 am. Gorton said he had probably arrived at the Embassy at 'a quarter to 12 or 12 o'clock or sometime later.'

Then on 21 March 1969, Geraldine Willesee (daughter of Senator Don Willesee, later External Affairs Minister in the Whitlam Government, and sister of journalist Mike Willesee) issued a statutory declaration giving details of the episode and saying Gorton had declared as he left the Press Gallery dinner: 'This girl is coming with me.'

Gorton was forced to concede he had misled the House about the various times, but said the Lodge records showed he had returned there from the US Embassy at 3 am, having dropped Ms Willesee off at the flat she shared with her father. He simply never could appreciate how he became entrapped in such political mire. As for the media's role, in hindsight it can well be asked why members of the Press Gallery, including even Ms Willesee, who worked for the agency *Australia United Press*, did not report these goings on at the time? I can speak only for myself. I was at the Gallery dinner.

This was an era when an 'off-the-record' convention that applied to a Press Gallery dinner—meaning nothing that was said or done was reported—was observed. In more recent years, of course, this custom has been disregarded and one speech in particular by a Prime Minister—Paul Keating—rightly has become the stuff of reported political history. Back in 1969, the after-dinner events involving a prime minister only really became a headline story when they were made an issue in Parliament.

I wrote in a column published the day after the statutory declaration by Geraldine Willesee: 'My recollection is that I left the dinner at about 1 am. At that time the Prime Minister was still there. I have no knowledge of what happened after that.'

I did not know at the time that Gorton was going on to the US Embassy and I did not know there had been phone calls from the US Ambassador. Geraldine Willesee said in her statutory declaration that it was not until she was departing in Gorton's car that Eggleton told Gorton the Ambassador had just telephoned and suggested the Prime Minister drop in for a nightcap.

When the rumours did start to surface, most Press Gallery members, myself included, took the 'so-what' view

that whatever had happened after the dinner it was a
private matter. It was not until St John claimed in
Parliament that Gorton had prejudiced Australia-US
relations by taking a 19-year-old female reporter to the US
Embassy with him in the middle of the night that the
episode became a firm story.

The response from two of Gorton's old Labor opponents
in the Senate also was interesting. Don Willesee asked what
the fuss was about, and said any young reporter worth her
salt would take the opportunity to be with the US
Ambassador and the Prime Minister. He added: 'Most
parents would like their daughters escorted like that at
night.' Lionel Murphy, Leader of the Labor Opposition in
the Senate, made a statement in the Senate, which said in
part: 'I accept without reservation the statement of the
Prime Minister that his conduct has been entirely proper.
Will the Leader of the Government (in the Senate) accept
that while we differ with the Prime Minister on public
affairs we will not seek to displace him or injure him on the
basis of matters which even if true—which they are
not—have no relation to his public office.'

Meanwhile in that arena of public affairs, Whitlam was
getting Gorton's measure. He found it hard to better Gorton
on policy, since both men were centrists, so he turned to
humour and ridicule. At this Whitlam became a master, not
least because often all he had to do was quote Gorton back,
as with this statement by Gorton on health insurance
rebates: 'On the other hand, the AMA agrees with us, or I
believe will agree with us, that it is its policy and will be its
policy to inform patients who ask what the common fee is
and what their own fee is so that a patient will know
whether he is going to be operated on, if that is what it is,
on the basis of the common fee or not.'

Yet it was Gorton's Liberal colleagues who finally

brought him down: first by undermining him after the 1969 election (in which the Government's majority was slashed from 39 to seven in a 7.1 per cent swing to Labor) at the initial challenge led by David Fairbairn and McMahon, which Gorton narrowly survived in a party room ballot; and then at the climactic tussle that involved Fraser and McMahon in March 1971.

In this the media, initially *The Bulletin* and the Sydney *Daily Telegraph*, played a significant role. The controversy began with reports of serious dissension between the Army and Fraser, then Defence Minister, over its civil action programme in Vietnam. It grew when Gorton called in the Chief of the General Staff, Sir Thomas Daly, to assure him the Army had the Government's complete trust. It snowballed when Fraser resigned from the Cabinet, claiming Gorton had been disloyal to him and saying Gorton was not 'fit to hold the great office of Prime Minister'. And it was embellished by a dramatic incident in the House when journalist Alan Ramsey, then with *The Australian*, interrupted Gorton's convoluted version of events with an emotional shout from the Press Gallery: 'You liar!'

Inevitably, McMahon moved against Gorton for the second time, in the Liberal Party room on 10 March. On a confidence motion, the vote was tied at 33-33. The scene was described by Liberal participants as tense and emotional, with McMahon sitting to one side, pretending he was aloof from it all. John Gorton gave his casting vote against himself, declaring the leadership vacant. In a scenario that could have come out of a Gilbert and Sullivan opera, McMahon easily beat Billy Snedden for the leadership and thus the prime ministership. Ever a little different, Gorton then stood against Fairbairn and Fraser for the deputy leadership, won comfortably, and when offered a choice of portfolios by McMahon, took Defence.

This strange mix soon became a recipe for instability. McMahon-Gorton aggravation came to a head when Gorton wrote a series of articles for the now defunct *Sunday Australian* newspaper, entitled 'I Did It My Way'. These basically were in answer to lengthy criticism of him in a book, *The Gorton Experiment*, by Alan Reid, but Gorton's response contained many swipes at members of the McMahon Government. McMahon forced him to resign from the Ministry in August 1971.

As a backbencher on his way out, Gorton continued to hold hospitable court to his dwindling band of still-devoted followers and a few journalists in his room, U113, on the upper level in Old Parliament House, about as far away as he could be from the Prime Minister's suite. Regular attendees included Jim Killen and Margaret Guilfoyle, *Canberra Times* journalist David Solomon (later Press Secretary to Whitlam) and me.

Gorton spent much of his time cheerfully honing his dislike not so much of McMahon but of Malcolm Fraser. At one stage there was even a 'Bring Back Gorton' movement started in Melbourne. He pointedly resigned from the Liberal Party when Fraser took the leadership from Snedden in a 1975 party room coup. He later stood, unsuccessfully, for a Senate seat in the ACT as an Independent, directing his preferences to Labor.

It was at this point that another delightful little incident occurred. Gorton came to my office in Old Parliament House and asked me if I could get him into the Press Gallery in the House of Representatives, on the grounds he was writing several articles for newspapers at the time. He said he did not want to sit in the so-called Speaker's Gallery (which by convention he had the right to do at any time) because (a) that required a formal approach to the government led by Fraser, and (b) he would have been seated on the floor of the House. Instead, he said, he wanted to 'look down and see what that bastard Fraser is up to these days'. I got him temporary membership of the Press Gallery and on three occasions he sat next to me through Question Time, in the seat reserved for *The* (Adelaide) *Advertiser* representative.

After his wife Bettina died in 1983, John Gorton was a lonely figure in Canberra, and could often be seen walking with his dog in Manuka village or doing his weekend shopping at the Fyshwick markets. He was always ready to stop for a yarn with anyone who approached him. Visitors to Canberra, particularly those from overseas, were always amazed that this was a former prime minister, wandering and mingling, safely and alone, with no security men in tow. In 1993 he took on a new lease of life at the age of 81 when he remarried. His second wife was Nancy Home, widow of Commander Ian Macgregor, an officer on HMAS *Voyager* who died in the 1964 collision with HMAS *Melbourne*.

As an old man, Gorton much preferred Andrew Peacock to John Howard as Liberal leader, but agreed to be rehabilitated back into the Liberal Party in the late 1990s when it was headed by Howard. In July 1999 the main Administration Building in Canberra was renamed the Sir John Gorton Building by Howard.

In September of 2001 he was guest of honour at a Sydney dinner to mark his 90th birthday, at which the official eclectic hosts were Doug Anthony, former Labor Minister Clyde Cameron, and Tom Hughes, QC, who had been Gorton's Attorney-General. The dinner, in the Grand Ballroom of the *Hotel Westin*, was organised, efficiently as ever, by Ainsley Gotto. The only notable absent living Liberal from the old Gorton era on that night of nostalgia was Malcolm Fraser.

Gorton, though physically frail, made a good speech.

But the most fascinating part came when master-of-ceremonies Alan Jones read out a speech Gorton had made at a local hall at a place called Mystic Park in rural Victoria in April 1946. The occasion had been a welcome-home dinner after World War II for 17 local returned servicemen, including himself, and a tribute to one local, a Bob Davey, who had not returned.

The Gorton speech of 1946 to the local people in the Mystic Park hall ended this way: 'I want you to forget it is I who am standing here. And I want you to see instead Bob Davey. And behind him I want you to see an army, regiment on regiment of young men, dead. They say to you, "burning in tanks and aeroplanes, drowning in submarines, shattered and broken by high explosive shells, we gave the last full measure of devotion. We bought your freedom with our lives. So take this freedom. Guard it as we have guarded it. Use it as we can no longer use it, and with it as a foundation, build. Build a world in which meanness and poverty, tyranny and hate, have no existence." If you see and hear these men behind me—do not fail them.'

It is not recorded how the Mystic Park people reacted to that speech in 1946. But in 2001 at Gorton's 90th birthday party there was a spontaneous standing ovation when Alan Jones read it out. Gorton had made that speech three years before he went into Parliament. He was not doing anything more than saying what he felt. He obviously had no speechwriter. Clearly there was no convolution. Guests at his 90th birthday commented it was the finest speech he had ever made.

It was sad that Gorton never did have a reconciliation with Malcolm Fraser, who had lobbied to get him into the prime ministership in 1968. It was also sad, and unnecessary, that Tom Hughes should wait all those years to launch into a vitriolic attack on Fraser, sitting in the congregation, at Gorton's funeral in 2002.

When Gorton retired from Parliament before the 1972 election, a small group of us in the Press Gallery took him to lunch at the *Bacchus Tavern* in Canberra's Civic Centre. It was a convivial affair in which many events of his unusual period as Prime Minister were mulled over at great length. At about 5 pm, Gorton said: 'Should we go now, or wait for the traffic to clear?' Canberra, of course, had virtually no peak hour traffic.

At about 6 pm, he said: 'The traffic has probably cleared. What say we stay and have a drink before dinner?' The lunch-cum-dinner lasted well into the night. To the end, 'Jolly John' Grey Gorton did it his way.

McMahon

HIS OWN WORST ENEMY

William McMahon, Liberal (1971–72)
1 year, 8 months and 25 days.

'There comes a time in the life of a man in the flood of time that taken at the flood leads on to fortune.'

McMahon, trying to quote Shakespeare's Julius Caesar, *at the White House, October 1971*

'He was determined, like other little Caesars, to destroy the member for Higgins (John Gorton). There he sat, on the Isle of Capri at Surfers Paradise, plotting his destruction—Tiberius with a telephone.'

Gough Whitlam

Bill McMahon, the first non-Victorian Liberal Prime Minister, came to the nation's most powerful office on that extraordinary March day in 1971 at the age of 63 with half the federal parliamentary Liberal Party—his detractors who were Gorton supporters—worried he would be a catastrophe. The other half, his backers, desperately hoped he would live up to the image of the persistent dapper 'little pro' he projected, pull the Coalition Government out of its deep doldrums and halt what was seen as the inexorable Whitlam progress.

For example, Queensland Liberal MP Kevin Cairns, one of McMahon's supporters, reflected initial high hopes for the new Prime Minister when he said: 'John Gorton is a loveable larrikin, but what we need now is a professional.'

Ironically, it was on the day after the Liberal leadership change that Gorton gave probably his best performance in the House. In a speech that was unusually precise and cogent, Gorton managed to subtly flay both Malcolm Fraser and David Fairbairn and pledge his support to the McMahon-led Government at the same time. This prompted Labor frontbencher Fred Daly to call out to a nervous Coalition: 'There's prime ministerial potential in your ranks at last... John Gorton!'

McMahon, by contrast, managed to make his first speech to the House as Prime Minister one of his worst and most disjointed. It was an inauspicious beginning for the fourth Liberal Prime Minister in five years.

On the one hand he was a veteran, one of the Class of '49 that had swept into office under Menzies, and so had experience. He also had powerful backers, including the non-Labor Premiers and Sydney media baron Sir Frank Packer. He was independently wealthy. He had a beautiful socialite wife, Sonia, 24 years his junior, whom he had married in 1965 at the age of 57. He had degrees in economics and law from Sydney University.

He had finally overcome the McEwen veto and had survived the McEwen juggernaut. He had held to his free-trading policy line. He had been recognised as a good Treasurer—though he was not as adept as he made out when he rattled off a bewildering array of economic facts and figures in Parliament, only to find his staff frequently had to call in *Hansard* to correct his speeches for the public record.

On the other hand McMahon was trusted by virtually none of his peers. In the recent past, McEwen and Hasluck had made that very clear. Further back, Menzies had his doubts about McMahon's trust-worthiness, though never about his energy or enthusiasm. Gorton obviously distrusted him. So did Jim Killen. McMahon likewise trusted few of his colleagues.

His official public service advisers, such as Sir John Bunting, who he brought back from obscurity and reappointed as Secretary of the Prime Minister's Department, and Dr HC ('Nugget') Coombs, who he made his 'unofficial guru', did their professional best for him. But among many he neither dispensed nor was able to command any significant loyalty.

At the same time, Whitlam's momentum continued to mount. All the symbolism and imagery was against McMahon in such a contest: a tall, confident imposing figure versus an often nervous 'Little Billy' with big ears, who Killen once said looked 'like a Volkswagen with its doors open'; a witty and imperious Opposition Leader who knew his time was coming, versus the Liberals' last-choice Prime Minister at his wit's end, whose time was running out; the giant versus the dwarf.

McMahon's first serious mistake as Prime Minister was not long in coming and was one of his worst: he owed favours to too many MPs who had voted for him and so rewarded them with Ministerial portfolios. Though one of these was highly deserved—Kevin Cairns, a former dentist with sound economic credentials—in the reshuffling process McMahon dropped Killen as Navy Minister without explanation.

Removed from the discipline of the convention of ministerial solidarity, Killen was free to criticise McMahon as he saw fit. Spurred on by antagonism to him by the Queensland Liberal Party executive and its president Eric Robinson, and by their support for McMahon against Gorton, Killen declared: 'They'll need a firing squad to silence me.' He flayed McMahon frequently, cleverly and mercilessly in speeches and newspaper articles.

Fred Daly used to delight in telling the story of Killen's apocryphal response in the House when McMahon, in answering a question from the Opposition, said: 'Mr Speaker, I know I am my own worst enemy.' Killen, from the backbench: 'Not while I'm alive, you're not.'

Killen enjoyed behind-the-scenes empathy with Whitlam (later to become genuine friendship when both had retired) in a bond marked by their love of words. When McMahon's appointee, Dr Malcolm Mackay, a Presbyterian cleric, succeeded Killen as Navy Minister, Whitlam drily observed in Parliament: 'The new man is of lesser calibre than his predecessor but a bigger bore.'

The underlying tensions in the Liberal ranks caused by the McMahon-Gorton rift never dissipated, neither before McMahon sacked Gorton as Defence Minister in August 1971 nor afterwards. At one stage there were eight former Ministers on the Coalition backbench: Gorton, Killen, Tom Hughes (former Attorney-General), 'Bert' Kelly (former Works Minister), Leslie Bury (former Foreign Affairs Minister and Treasurer under Gorton), Sir John Cramer (former Army Minister), Sir Charles Adermann (former Primary Industry Minister) and Dudley Erwin (former Air Minister).

The rumblings beneath the wafer-thin veneer of Coalition calm prompted Arthur Calwell, then 75 and walking with the aid of two sticks, to make a quip to a Liberal minister in King's Hall which reverberated around the lobbies: 'Yours is the only ruling party we have ever seen with a shadow Cabinet.'

Nor did the policy differences between McMahon and the Country Party disappear with the departure of McEwen. In drama reminiscent of the row over devaluation of the dollar between Holt and McEwen in December of 1967, in December of 1971, the Liberals and the Country Party were similarly convulsed.

The USA, finally unable to absorb the cost of the Vietnam War, devalued its dollar by 8.5 per cent. The Treasury, backed by McMahon, wanted to revalue the Australian dollar fully by 8.5 per cent and in line with sterling. The Trade Department, backed by McEwen's successor as Country Party leader and deputy Prime Minister, Doug Anthony, wanted full devaluation in line with the US dollar.

Cabinet was deadlocked. Anthony at one stage was reported to have threatened to take the Country Party out of the Coalition. McMahon, claiming there had been no compromise, eventually announced there would be a revaluation of 6.32 per cent. In retrospect the argument seems minor. But it was a big, public and acrimonious argument at the time, and was written up as such, much to the detriment of the image of the Government.

McMahon's penchant for the telephone was as insatiable when he became Prime Minister as it had been beforehand. He was a telephone addict. He loved to gossip. The sobriquet 'Billy the Leak' was apt. All the massive amount of anecdotal evidence indicates he was seldom off the phone, whatever the hour of the day or night: to businessmen at the top end of town, with whom he had considerable rapport; to political colleagues as he sought to garner support; to newspaper proprietors and editors as he tried to mould public opinion; and to members of the Press Gallery so he could reveal news snippets casting himself, inevitably, in a favourable light.

The telephone addict at work, and play.

McMahon, of course, was not alone in this habit. There are few MPs who do not indulge in selective favourable 'leaks'. The habit is not necessarily bad. Indeed if a leak rights a wrong or reveals an error or misdeed, it obviously is beneficial. Indeed in that era there were at least two notable, deliberate and most worthy leakers of information—one Labor and the other Liberal. They took the view, obviously a proper one in the view of the media, that in the Australian democracy people had the right to know what was being discussed in the government or opposition party rooms by their elected representatives as decisions that would affect them were being made. They also realised that attempts to keep such discussions and decisions secret were pointless anyway.

One was Queenslander Ron McAuliffe, who was more famous as president and father figure of Rugby League in that State and the person who initiated the annual State-of-Origin competition. McAuliffe was a Labor Senator from 1971 to 1981. Invariably after a Labor caucus meeting he would make himself available to a few journalists, either in his room or openly in the corridor, and, without self-aggrandisement, tell them what had happened.

The other was Les Irwin, the Liberal MP for the NSW seat of Mitchell from 1963 to 1972. He was even more assiduous than McAuliffe. He had such a penchant for accuracy that he always took a newspaper, *The Daily Telegraph*, into the party room and made notes on it in shorthand. In his room later, he would say to the few journalists who always consulted him: 'Well, you may as well get it right,' and then open his newspaper and read his notes from it.

Some of McAuliffe and Irwin's colleagues who knew (or suspected) what they were doing could become quite angry. But their open attitude led eventually to an entirely appropriate and welcome change, in which the major parties appointed spokespeople to officially brief the media (albeit often selectively) on party room debates and decisions.

Bill McMahon, however, was in a different league. He was undoubtedly the grand master of the art of the often-devious leak. There was one notable occasion, for instance, when I had just returned with my family on a Sunday night to our Canberra home after a weekend at Bateman's Bay. It was about 10 pm and the phone was ringing as we walked in the door. 'Is that you, Wally?' came the familiar sing-song voice (he hardly ever began a phone call with revelation of his name), 'I wanted to let you know that the Cabinet had a special meeting today on the Seas and Submerged Lands Bill [an issue of much contention with the States] and I persuaded the others this is what we should tell the Premiers when we meet...'

He went on for another 15 minutes or so. I thanked him and promptly phoned the story, using the ubiquitous phrase 'senior government sources said', to *The Courier-Mail*. The story was page one news in the newspaper next morning—as it was in several other newspapers, with but slight variations. Clearly I had not been the only journalist the Prime Minister had phoned.

The Premiers were angry: (a) at the thrust of the story; and (b) that they had read it first in the newspapers rather than from the Commonwealth Government in conference with them. The following night the phone rang again, also at about 10 pm, just as I got home from my Parliament House office. 'Wally, it's Bill McMahon here' (this time he used his name and there was a barely discernible laugh), 'I wanted to let you know that I was absolutely appalled today at the way that story leaked from the Cabinet and I really hauled my Ministers over the coals.'

However, there were—at least—two occasions where McMahon's late-night use of the phone rebounded. One story has it that when he was Labour and National Service Minister he did not finish reading his Cabinet briefing documents until about 2.30 am, and then telephoned the Secretary of his Department, Sir Henry Bland, seeking more information on some questions. Bland promptly and politely obliged, went to work, and phoned McMahon back two hours later, no doubt waking him from what must have been a sound sleep by that time.

On the other occasion, McMahon as Prime Minister rang public service mandarin Sir Frederick Wheeler, then

Secretary of the Treasury, after midnight, getting Wheeler out of bed, and requesting detailed information urgently on a particular issue. As related to me later by what might be called a 'senior public service source', Wheeler concealed his annoyance and asked when the Prime Minister wanted the information. 'As soon as possible', was the reply.

Wheeler promptly set to the task, waking two other senior public servants in the process. At about 2.30 am he phoned McMahon at The Lodge, disturbing him from a deep slumber. Angrily, McMahon said: 'Why did you wake me at this dreadful hour?' 'Because', said Wheeler innocently, 'You wanted the information as soon as possible, and I have it now.' McMahon was understood (according to the same 'senior public service source'), never to have phoned Wheeler outside normal office hours again.

For McMahon, realisation of the prime ministerial dream which had been his goal for so long turned out to be a nightmare. He had a long record of service behind him. Yet having built a reputation of always being on top of his many ministerial portfolios (Navy and Air, Social Services, Primary Industry, Labour and National Service, and External Affairs, as well as the Treasury), McMahon found himself in all sorts of difficulties in the top job. Perhaps Labor's Eddie Ward had been the first to realise McMahon was often a square peg in a round hole. On McMahon's appointment as Primary Industry Minister in 1956—which was taken by many Liberals as a Menzies' joke at the expense of the Country Party—Ward scoffed: 'The only thing the new Minister knows about agriculture is how to water the pot plants in his Kings Cross flat.' McMahon, for all his persistence and industriousness, simply was out of his depth as Prime Minister—and the tide was against him.

It was in the White House library in October 1971 that McMahon made his most publicised jumble. In retrospect it may seem trivial to categorise the incident as a blunder, but it was symptomatic of the McMahon problem. He had just been officially welcomed to the US by President Richard Nixon, who had advanced into the glare of the television lights and delivered a smooth speech off-the-cuff, or at least one without notes. McMahon, trusting in his own memory, decided he should extemporise also and put aside his prepared speech: 'I take as my text a few familiar words,' he began, trying to remember Brutus' assertion in Julius Caesar, 'There comes a time in the life of a man in the flood of time that taken at the flood leads on to fortune...'

Australian Embassy officials groaned. Journalists laughed. 'Oh, God', said one Australian reporter audibly, 'I wish I were an Italian'. The damage was done. Though McMahon's visit to the USA proved valuable, to the extent that he established considerable rapport with US business leaders, he was remembered by State Department officials several years later mainly for that faux pas. He was also remembered for the dramatic picture Sonia presented when she wore a revealing evening gown, split to her upper thigh, to a dinner at the White House hosted by Nixon.

In a matter of more serious foreign policy—relations with mainland China—McMahon also miscued, basically because the Nixon Administration had not told him of its latest diplomatic moves—much to the delight of Gough Whitlam. In April 1971, when Australia still did not recognise China diplomatically, Whitlam cabled the formidable Chinese Premier Chou En-Lai, suggesting a visit by an Australian Labor Party delegation. In May he received a reply from the Chinese People's Institute of Foreign Affairs (the body used by China for contacts with non-recognising nations) saying this would be welcome.

The Whitlam-led party included the ALP federal president Tom Burns of Queensland, ALP federal secretary

Mick Young of South Australia, the party's primary industry spokesman, Dr Rex Patterson of Queensland, Whitlam's superb speechwriter and general factotum Graham Freudenberg, and several journalists (including Laurie Oakes but not me, as I had contracted mumps) who had been accepted at the last minute by the Chinese. This party arrived in Beijing early in July 1971 from Hong Kong.

The highlight was an extensive well-publicised meeting between Whitlam and Chou En-Lai on how to improve China-Australia relations. It was held in the Great Hall of the People on 5 July, in front of Chinese officials and the Australian journalists. *Australian Associated Press* correspondent David Barnett, later press secretary to Malcolm Fraser when he was Prime Minister and later still John Howard's official biographer, took a full shorthand note.

Whitlam denigrated Harold Holt's 'All the Way with LBJ' policy on Vietnam, said the American people would force US policy to change on Vietnam, and stressed Labor's policy was for Australia to recognise one China with Beijing as the sole capital. The worldly, sophisticated and Paris-educated Chou praised Whitlam for his perception. It was the first meeting between a Western political leader and the Beijing Government since Britain's Lord Attlee's visit in the 1950s.

At home, McMahon reacted instinctively, backed by the old Rightist leader of the Democratic Labor Party leader, Senator Vince Gair of Queensland, and by the National Civic Council head Mr BA Santamaria. 'We must not become the pawns of the giant Communist power in our region', McMahon declared on 12 July. 'In no time at all, Mr Chou had Mr Whitlam on a hook and he played him as a fisherman plays a trout.'

However, on 15 July, President Nixon announced that as a result of secret talks in Beijing between Chou En-Lai and US Secretary of State Henry Kissinger, he had accepted an invitation to visit China to establish a better US-China relationship. Kissinger had actually been in Beijing at the same time as Whitlam.

Whitlam's deputy Lance Barnard, who was acting Labor leader during his absence, best summed up the situation with his description of McMahon as a 'stunned mullet'. To mix the metaphor, McMahon came across as a lame duck when all he could say of the Nixon-Kissinger initiative was: 'It's our policy too'. Whitlam had been lucky in the timing of his visit to China and a reactive McMahon had taken the hit. From that point McMahon toned down his anti-China rhetoric and began to refer to 'Continental China' and 'Taiwan China'. And as the USA realised it was losing the Vietnam War and started to withdraw troops, so did the McMahon Government start to pull back Australian forces.

When the UN General Assembly overwhelmingly expelled Taiwan from its membership in October 1971 (against a minority which included the USA and Australia) and gave the seat to China instead, the McMahon Government said it would move cautiously towards diplomatic recognition of China. But it made a point of still officially calling Taiwan 'The Republic of China'.

Inevitably, as 1971 dragged on into 1972, it was not McMahon, but Whitlam and the Labor Party, as a genuinely perceived alternative government, who either grabbed or were given the more positive headlines by the media. One particular example was Labor's final and formal abandonment, at a party Conference, of the White Australia policy it had originally implemented at the turn of the century. This was carried, by 44 votes to one (that of 'old guard' Fred Daly) on a motion by one of South Australia's most notable and liberal-minded Premiers, Don Dunstan, that Australia's immigration policy would be based on 'the avoidance of discrimination on any grounds of race, or colour of skin, or nationality.'

Though Holt's Government in 1966 had been the first to abandon such discrimination, though it was Dunstan who constantly prodded the ALP more than anyone, it was Gough Whitlam in Opposition in 1971 who got most of the credit. Another significant example was a Labor policy decision to accelerate independence for Papua New Guinea, a subject long dear to Whitlam's heart. Again, because the tide was with Labor, this was recognised by the media to be the policy of the next Australian Government, and again McMahon could do little more than react.

Indeed, to his credit McMahon did react positively by appointing Andrew Peacock as External Territories Minister with a brief to advance self-government for Papua New Guinea. This Peacock did, striking up a rapport with Michael Somare, who was to become the former colony's first Prime Minister. Yet in the perception of most Australians even this move by McMahon appeared to do little more than validate Whitlam's initiatives.

At the same time, McMahon abandoned Gorton's Offshore legislation, to the delight of the Liberal Premiers and the consternation of Gorton's Liberal backers in federal Parliament.

The image of a government in turmoil further intensified when McMahon, on the eve of his departure for Washington, denied reports the USA had asked Australia to help train Cambodian troops, just as it had helped train South Vietnamese troops in the early 1960s. It soon became clear, however that the US Embassy in Canberra had made such a request but Defence Minister David Fairbairn, inexplicably and inexcusably, had not told him.

Further signs that McMahon was floundering in international waters came during a goodwill trip to South-East Asia in June 1972, when he first told President Suharto of Indonesia that Australia was a 'West European' nation and that discussion about it being part of Asia was too philosophical a question. This when Suharto had given McMahon a full ceremonial welcome and opened the door for McMahon to stress Australia's links with Asia.

Then, in a bid to placate Suharto, McMahon said he did not really see the need for the Five-Power defence agreement (between Australia, Britain, Malaysia, Singapore and New Zealand), which managed to upset Lee Kuan Yew of Singapore and Malaysian Prime Minister Tun Razak no end.

On his chartered Qantas aircraft coming back from Asia, McMahon told journalists he wished he had been better understood in Singapore and Indonesia, but blamed diplomatic advisers for not briefing him properly. I wrote a column on 'McMahon's slippery dip travels'.

Finally the phoney election war, won convincingly by Whitlam at just about every turn, ended, and the 1972 election campaign proper came around. It was time for the great conservative Australian electorate to put this conservative Coalition out of its misery. The campaign by McMahon, outwardly cheerful and oblivious to the impending doom, was a disaster.

'My Government will murder the Labor Party at the federal elections, we will murder the brutes,' he happily told 500 barn-dancers in a fruit-picking shed in Victoria. 'Never in the history of Liberal Government, whether with Sir Robert Menzies, Harold Holt or Gorton, I believe that in the past 14 to 16 months we have carried out a series of reforms that have never been equalled.'

Liberal and Labor MPs and journalists alike on the campaign trail scratched their heads. Some cynics in the Press Gallery gleefully recalled an equally fatuous statement McMahon had made on the ABC's *This Day Tonight* programme in June 1971: 'Admittedly, I can't go too far and tell you explicitly what we have done because I think if I did it would undo all the good that has been achieved already.'

McMahon announced the election would be held on 2 December. Whitlam, skilfully continuing to employ the politics of ridicule and laughter, responded: 'The Prime Minister has steadfastly adhered to the principle he announced for himself on this subject last March: "What I have never done is to fix a date until I have made up my mind what the date is likely to be."'

Whitlam continued: 'The Second of December is a memorable day. It is the anniversary of Austerlitz. Far be it from me to wish, or appear to wish, to assume the mantle of Napoleon, but I cannot forget that the Second of December was a date on which a crushing defeat was administered to a coalition—another ramshackle, reactionary coalition.' With double entendre, Whitlam was later to thunder several times during the campaign: 'McMahon is no laughing matter.'

From the start, nothing seemed to go right for McMahon, and not the least of his worries was the realisation that Rupert Murdoch had recently bought the Sydney *Daily Telegraph* from avowed Liberal supporter Sir Frank Packer. Partly influenced by John Menadue, a former private secretary to Whitlam who had become News Ltd general manager in Australia (and who later had an even more distinguished career as Secretary of the Prime Minister's Department under both Whitlam and Fraser, then as Ambassador to Japan and head of Qantas), Murdoch had committed his newspapers editorially to a change of Government.

At the same time Whitlam snaffled the legendary 'Nugget' Coombs, and announced Coombs would be his personal economic adviser. Labor's general secretary Mick Young masterminded the 'It's Time' campaign and brought many Catholics, lost to Labor since the great party Split of 1954, back into the fold. Most notable was Archbishop James Carroll of Sydney, who said Labor's education policy would be acceptable to Catholics.

'I ask you to study our record and vote Labor,' McMahon said haplessly on one occasion on the campaign trail. 'We will honour all our promises on the problems we have made,' he said on another.

Besieged on all sides, McMahon's worst campaign moments came in Brisbane. Having launched officially with a clinical pre-recorded televised address, he decided to go 'live' to an audience of supporters in the Brisbane City Hall. He used an autocue, at that time an unsophisticated partly hand-driven device, from which he read his speeches. Worse, he used one that did not work properly. Adhering firmly to his script and refusing to ad-lib or reply to interjections, McMahon at first spoke at a measured pace, then quickly, then slowly, then softly, then louder and louder.

It was a truly dreadful performance—the explanation for which came when an enterprising reporter, Sally-Anne Atkinson, later Liberal Lord Mayor of Brisbane, went behind scenes. She found the technician responsible for the autocue was having terrible trouble getting the machine to run smoothly and to compensate had turned the volume up... and up.

Yet even that effort was not as devastating for McMahon's colleagues, particularly his Ministers, as a radio interview he gave in Brisbane about a week before polling day. In it he said he did not trust his Cabinet to make the right decisions. Said McMahon: 'I have learnt that I now must make more decisions than I had the intention of making when I first became the Prime Minister. I wanted to be the head of a team. I wanted to delegate the authority to the relevant Minister... I couldn't get the work done quickly enough and I found frequently that the political approaches to it were not as good as I thought they should be.'

Those were the words of a desperate man. The 'little pro' of yore had become very amateurish. He had made himself a major poll issue. He was lampooned by cartoonists. In Queensland the National Party ran a full-page advertisement in *The Courier-Mail*: 'While Australia searches for a leader, Queensland has found Joh Bjelke-Petersen.'

Yet surprisingly to many, and in contrast to the perception now prevalent through the rose-coloured glasses of history Whitlam who, of course, had already captured a swag of Liberal seats in 1969, did not win that 1972 general election in a landslide. His victory was not like the 74-to-47 seats sweep into office that Menzies had enjoyed in 1949. McMahon did not lose by all that much.

Despite all the justifiable atmospherics, Labor had a net gain of only eight seats across Australia—winning six in New South Wales, four in Victoria, one in Queensland and one in Tasmania; and losing one seat in Victoria, one in South Australia and two in Western Australia.

Labor's proportion of the total two-party-preferred vote was still less than half, at 49.6 per cent. It finished with a relatively slim nine-seat majority in the House of Representatives, 67 seats to 58. But a win is a win is a win, and Whitlam grandly claimed his mandate.

There were basically three reasons for the relatively small defeat of McMahon: (a) the fact that Labor under Whitlam had already chopped the Coalition majority from 39 to seven seats in the 1969 election campaign against Gorton; (b) the business community basically stuck with McMahon; and (c) the Australian economy was still healthy and stable (though over-heating, as Whitlam was to discover). The unemployment rate was a mere 1.46 per cent. Only 82 400 people in a workforce of about 5.5 million were registered as seeking jobs.

Years later, Whitlam, in his book *The Whitlam Government 1972-75*, made what could be seen as an attempt to explain why he had not crashed through as dramatically as he had anticipated. He was surprisingly generous to McMahon. 'It now tends to be forgotten,' said Whitlam, 'that McMahon was an extraordinarily skilful, resourceful and tenacious politician. Had he been otherwise, the ALP victory in December 1972 would have been even more convincing than it was.'

Horsefeathers! In that 1972 campaign, McMahon was neither skilful nor resourceful, nor tenacious. He stumbled at the highest hurdle in his career, and then crashed.

As 23 years of non-Labor rule came to an end, McMahon conceded defeat promptly and graciously at 11.30 pm on election night, and commented off-handedly immediately after: 'At least I didn't lose as many seats as Gorton.'

However, though defeated as Prime Minister, McMahon stayed in Parliament for another nine years, projecting the image of a party elder statesman, often criticising his own side of politics, maintaining his contacts with business leaders, and still constantly phoning journalists. But by then nobody was really listening. When the Liberals returned to power in 1975, Malcolm Fraser, understandably, could find no room for McMahon.

In the 1977 election McMahon puzzled everyone, and not least Jim Killen, by asking him to open his campaign in his Sydney seat of Lowe. Killen duly obliged.

McMahon was knighted, on Fraser's recommendation, in 1977, and he was the last of Menzies' famous '49-ers to leave Parliament when he resigned in early 1982. Sadly and undeservedly for a man who had seen good times and bad times in a 33-year political career, he was a loser to the end. He caused a by-election in Lowe which the Liberal Party lost to Labor. He died in 1988 after a long battle with cancer.

Whitlam

CRASHING THROUGH

**Edward Gough Whitlam, Labor (1972–1975)
2 years, 11 months, and 7 days.**

'Brilliant, confident, he strode the political stage like a colossus about to realise his ambition to become Prime Minister of Australia.'

Fred Daly, veteran Labor MP, in his book
From Curtin to Hawke

'Comrades, the fun is where I am.'

*Whitlam, as Ambassador to UNESCO, in reply
to a question by Mungo MacCallum,
National Press Club, March 1984*

On 13 November 1972, there was a wondrous performance, a communion of faith and hope and hype, at the Blacktown Civic Centre in Sydney's ever-sprawling western suburbs. There was an atmosphere of anticipated euphoria that probably had not been matched before in Australian political history and certainly has not been seen since.

'Men and women of Australia,' Gough Whitlam began with evangelical fervour at the launch of his official policy speech, borrowing from John Curtin, 'Will you believe with me that Australia can be changed, should be changed, must be changed?... We are coming into government after 23 years in opposition...'.

And so it was duly ordained. And so on the following December 5, three days after polling day, his old political enemy, Governor-General Sir Paul Hasluck, over whom he had once tossed a glass of water in the House, duly administered the oath of office to Whitlam.

One of the first to congratulate him was Sir Robert Menzies, by telegram. Whitlam replied, 'You would, I think, be surprised to know how much I feel indebted to your example, despite the great differences in our philosophies. In particular, your remarkable achievement in re-building your own party and bringing it so triumphantly to power within six years has been an abiding inspiration to me.'

So began the most exciting, hasty, ambitious, unpredictable, innovative, tumultuous, erratic and news-packed term of any Australian government. An impatient Whitlam believed he should have become Prime Minister three years earlier. He described the years 1969-72 as a 'kind of interregnum'. Having finally made it, from the very beginning he was in hurry, riding shotgun in his avowed partnership with the people. He refused to wait for the final counts in marginal seats and thus for confirmation of the full membership of the Labor Caucus which would formally choose the new Ministers. Whitlam formed a remarkable duumvirate with his deputy Lance Barnard, allotting himself 13 ministerial portfolios and Barnard 14, including that of Defence Minister, which was always understood would be Barnard's sole portfolio when the full Ministry was finally appointed on 19 December.

Amazing everybody, not least Hasluck and the public service chiefs who had facilitated an admirable transition to the new regime without visible rancour of any sort, the two-man Whitlam Ministry made 40 decisions in its two weeks of existence. Some of these decisions included the ending of conscription, the freeing of draft resisters from jail, diplomatic recognition of China and the ending of recognition of Taiwan. He also withdrew the remaining Australian troops from Vietnam and Cambodia (most, including the conscripts, had come home 15 months earlier and virtually all that remained of Australia's military presence by December 1972 was a unit to protect the Australian Embassy in Saigon).

For all these momentous decisions Whitlam was able to claim he had a detailed mandate, since they had all been proposed in his policy speech. Yet in his hurry to assume the reins of office, he made what were later seen to be two mistakes. The first was to create the impression that he was determined to change everything, which innately conservative Australians, and especially the business community, did not want. The second was to omit Labor's Senate leader, an upset Lionel Murphy, and deputy Senate leader Don Willesee, from his first Ministry. Whitlam took the view that the Senate and its members were not as important as Members of the House of Representatives—an assessment he could never acknowledge was misguided, not even after it contributed to his downfall on 11 November 1975.

Whitlam was the most paradoxical of all prime ministers in the last half of the 20th century. A man of superb intellect, knowledge and literacy, he yet had little ability when it came to economics. An arrogant man of tall and imposing physique, he used his magnificent command of the language with excoriating skill against his opponents. Yet he had a sharp sense of humour and, for those who heard his pithy comments as distinct from those who only read them, a subtle and captivating ability to be self-mocking.

He worked at being a character and he succeeded. The title of Graham Freudenberg's splendid book about Whitlam, *A Certain Grandeur*, which was a phrase taken from a book by Clem Lloyd and Gordon Reid about the first term (1972-74) of the Whitlam Government, is appropriate.

Whitlam rivalled Menzies in his passion for the House of Representatives and ability to use it as his stage, and yet his parliamentary skills were rhetorical and not tactical. He could devise a strategy and then often botch the tactics in trying to implement that strategy. He was tactless. He was impetuous and infuriating and yet he could be charming. His encyclopaedic mind often dragged up minutiae as he quickly sought, and produced, the perfect one-liner.

He was a social builder and policy innovator but he failed to grasp that he could succeed in neither of these endeavours when the economic base eroded. He was an indefatigable worker. His mercurial temperament suited him better in Opposition than it did in Government. Above all he was a man of grand vision with serious blind spots. No Prime Minister has had so much written about him or written and lectured so much about himself and the controversies, which he either created or in which he became embroiled. The anecdotes appear endless as related by Daly, Killen, Freudenberg, and Barry Cohen.

Whitlam dragged the Labor Party screaming into the

1970s in the face of opposition from the 'Twelve Witless Men' of its executive—his first notorious tag, which almost resulted in his expulsion from the ALP in 1966. He changed the face of Australia, on balance for the better.

Whitlam was a joy to travel with. He went in great style at taxpayers' expense (with media representatives' companies footing their own expensive bills) to the most exotic places, many of them ruins of previous civilisations, as well as the world's current most civilised capitals. He stood on the ruins of Yucatan in 1975 and said to his party of officials and Press people: 'Stick around comrades, there'll be a lot more of this.' There wasn't.

In all circumstances he displayed what can only be described as a Presence with a capital P. At the start of every trip, with an idiosyncrasy borne out of his wartime years as an RAAF navigator, he would stop at the door of his VIP aircraft, take out a notebook, write down the flight number and the name of the flight commander, and inquire solicitously about his health. Thirty years later he was still doing this when he boarded civilian aircraft.

When he settled down in his seat, while others read books and newspapers and briefing notes, he often would pull out an old parliamentary *Hansard* and chuckle over debates of yesteryear—for relaxation!

His aplomb certainly stood him in good stead on one flight in particular, from Canberra to Wellington in an RAAF BAC-111 aircraft when, almost halfway across the Tasman Sea, one of its two engines stopped. As the aircraft slowed down markedly and banked into a wide turn, Whitlam looked behind to one of his accompanying advisers, Sir Arthur Tange, then Secretary of the Defence Department, and said: 'Tell me Arthur, do you have anyone in mind who might succeed you in Defence?'

When the aircraft skipper came back from the cockpit

to the aircraft's cabin, he told us we were turning back to Canberra and said: 'There's no problem, Prime Minister, these aircraft fly just as well on one engine as they do on two engines.' Whitlam responded with a smile: 'Thank you, Wing Commander, and tell me, do they fly as well on no engines as they do on one?' Whitlam's sense of fun in serious circumstances could be classic.

Though he was later to be remembered for innovative big-ticket items such as Medibank and native land rights and family law, one of his most passionate down-to-earth desires was to leave no urban house unsewered. This may have done more to get him into office than any other policy. His enthusiasm for this was borne out of the fact that he represented the south-western Sydney electorate of Cabramatta, which was largely unsewered and unsealed. This Whitlam passion gave birth to the Department of Urban and Regional Development when he came to power.

The Whitlam Government's zeal for grand publicly-funded development was so great that as early as 25 January 1973, it met with the Premiers of Victoria, Rupert Hamer, and New South Wales, Robin Askin, and relevant officials at Albury-Wodonga, and set aside an area with a radius of 55km. It was a sign of different times and less financial constraint that as Urban and Regional Development Minister, Tom Uren could announce simply: 'We all agreed to develop a new city there.'

At the same time as Whitlam was setting the pace in the federal Government—or more accurately, in legislative terms in the House of representatives, because Labor with only 26 Senators did not control the Senate—in Queensland there came the rise and rise of arch conservative and populist Sir Joh Bjelke-Petersen. Sir Joh, the National Party Premier, possessed no rhetorical skills but lots of native cunning. Ironically, it was Whitlam who made Bjelke-

Petersen a folk hero in parochial Queensland because all the latter really had to do was say 'no' when the former said 'yes' and 'yes' when Whitlam said 'no' and blame all perceived ills on this arrogant southern socialist who was changing everything.

However, Bjelke-Petersen knew he needed the dreaded Commonwealth's money and when Whitlam offered special funds for sewerage in Brisbane under a Commonwealth-Queensland Sewerage Agreement, he came to Canberra to sign it—albeit in a tense political atmosphere.

On 14 February 1975, I was in my Old Parliament House office, when Whitlam's Press Secretary David Solomon came in and said, deadpan: 'If you can spare a moment, Gough would like to see you in his office in half an hour to witness a document.' Intrigued, I turned up on time, and there were Whitlam and Bjelke-Petersen with a pile of papers in front of them. Bjelke-Petersen was surprised to see me in such an off-limits inner sanctum, but cordially and cautiously said 'hello'.

Said Whitlam, with a hearty chuckle: 'Comrade, Joh and I have this historic agreement to sign and we need a witness. It's St Valentine's Day and this is a sweetheart agreement on sewerage.' Only Whitlam would have thought of such a detailed offbeat scenario, and so to the bemusement of several government officials, anyone of whom could have been a witness, I added my signature to the Commonwealth-Queensland Sewerage Agreement beneath those of the Prime Minister and the Premier. The photo of this unusual event made page one in *The Courier-Mail* the next day.

Fun aside, Whitlam's period in office was marked by a series of events whose cumulative effect was to seriously damage his government. It was in January 1973, for example, that Sir Arthur Tange, in his role as Defence

Department Secretary, declared that Clem Lloyd, then press secretary to Defence Minister Lance Barnard, could not attend meetings with visiting British Defence Minister Lord Carrington for security reasons.

Barnard made the mistake of not overruling Tange on this, and Lloyd, who had been responsible for framing Labor's defence policy for the 1972 election, including the integration of the five services departments (Defence, Army, Navy, Air Force, and Supply) which Tange implemented, understandably was affronted and resigned. The Government realised too late that it had lost one of its most loyal staffers and astute political advisers. Lloyd switched to a successful career writing books and teaching journalism, and later became Professor of Journalism at Wollongong University.

This behind-scenes episode was followed at irregular and increasingly smaller intervals by a series of momentous and well-documented controversial events, which led to Whitlam's eventual downfall.

The first was on 16 March 1973 when Lionel Murphy as Attorney-General led a dramatic early-morning police raid, without Whitlam's knowledge, on the Melbourne headquarters of the Australian Security Intelligence Office. The bizarre reason Murphy gave was that he wanted to study the files relating to any possible Croatian terrorist moves against the Yugoslav Prime Minister Dzemal Bijedic, who was about to make a visit to Australia. Murphy was concerned that ASIO officers might remove or destroy such files.

Whether Murphy felt justified or not, this raid on a body for which he had ministerial responsibility was a Keystone Cops-type fiasco. It was to ever dog the Whitlam Government because it was so silly. It also overshadowed Murphy's impressive track record of legal and social reforms, which included establishment of legal aid, a Commonwealth Ombudsman, freedom of information legislation and the Family Law court.

Worse for Labor, the raid underlined the impression, which the Opposition seized on, that Murphy was a loose cannon in rivalry with Whitlam. This impression intensified as Murphy set about building up the Senate committee system, which in effect increased the already huge powers of the Senate—despite Labor's policy to abolish it. It was an investigative system, which the Liberal-National Coalition later was to use with devastating effect against Labor. It was the forerunner to the modern system in which some Senate committees, wrongly, assume more importance than the Senate itself.

The second major controversy came with the Gair Affair in the first half of 1974, in which Murphy also played a major part and blundered tactically. In a too-clever-by-half bid to get control of the Senate, Whitlam and Murphy secretly did a deal with Democratic Labor Party (DLP) leader and former ALP Premier of Queensland, Senator Vince Gair. The 73-year-old Gair wanted out, and Murphy saw a unique opportunity, with which Whitlam agreed. Gair was to become Ambassador to Ireland and thus create an extra Senate vacancy in Queensland (making the total six seats) which, under the proportional representation system, Labor could expect to win at a half-Senate election scheduled for May. Gair was duly formally appointed in March by Governor-General Hasluck and held his tongue.

However, Whitlam and Murphy made two mistakes. They failed to get Gair's resignation from the Senate in writing and they did not allow for the instant reactionary cunning of Liberal Senator Ian Wood of Mackay, Country Party leader Doug Anthony in Canberra and Bjelke-Petersen in Brisbane, when the news leaked out.

The story was broken by Laurie Oakes in the Melbourne *Sun News-Pictorial* on the morning of 2 April, the day Whitlam was due to make the announcement about Gair. Oakes had arrived in Canberra in January 1969, and this was his first big exclusive news story. The first hint came from a tip-off, that there was a key Senate development brewing of some sort, from John Lombard, who was Oakes' deputy. Lombard in turn had been tipped off by veteran radio journalist Frank Chamberlain, who was close to Whitlam.

I shared a small office in Old Parliament House with Oakes and other journalists in the old Herald and Weekly Times Ltd group, and could only admire his speculative late-night phone call—after hours of slotting pieces of the story together like a jigsaw puzzle—to the Gair's home in Brisbane, which finally gave him the confirmation he needed. When Mrs Gair answered the phone, Oakes said: 'I just want to congratulate the Senator on the ambassadorial appointment.' Mrs Gair replied: 'I'll pass it on. He will be very pleased. Thank you and goodnight.'

This public revelation of the Gair appointment by Oakes gave Whitlam's enemies the few hours they needed to work out a counter-manoeuvre to stop the Labor plan to win an extra Senate seat in Queensland, and Wood and Anthony separately phoned Bjelke-Petersen. It also led to what was dubbed by the media as the 'Night of the Long Prawns'.

Whitlam and Murphy suddenly realised they did not have Gair's resignation from the Senate, which is precisely what Wood and Anthony had told Bjelke-Petersen. But despite an intensive search by Labor staffers, they could not find Gair in the parliamentary building.

In fact he was one of a small group, which began with a threesome, in the office of genial Queensland Country Party Senator Ron Maunsell, supping on beer and Queensland banana prawns for several hours. Attacked by his

Democratic Labor Party colleagues, several Liberals and some Labor MPs alike, Gair had told Maunsell he was lonely and so Maunsell had taken him under his wing for the evening. Several Country Party MPs dropped in from time to time. Anthony called in briefly, had a beer and some prawns, and innocently asked Gair if he had handed in his resignation yet. Gair said he had it in his pocket and would resign from the Senate the following day.

In retrospect it is not clear that the wily Gair knew all the intricacies of what was happening elsewhere. He did not give the impression that he knew something big was brewing. He was enjoying himself, joking about his appointment to Dublin. Maunsell laughed about having Whitlam and Murphy 'with a bit of luck, by the short hairs'. Maunsell certainly knew what was happening elsewhere and he needed it to happen before Gair resigned from the Senate.

It was happening in Brisbane, where on Bjelke-Petersen's advice, the Queensland Governor, Sir Colin Hannah, was urgently issuing writs that night for the election of the five Queensland Senators whose terms were about to expire. This meant there could not be six Senate vacancies as planned by Whitlam and Murphy, because Gair's seat was not yet vacant. While the little party was proceeding in Maunsell's office, the Government Printer in Brisbane, on Bjelke-Petersen's order, was rushing off a special issue of the Queensland *Government Gazette*, proclaiming the issue of the Senate writs.

Sometime after midnight, when the Senate had risen for the night, and with the beer-and-prawns partygoers reduced to the original threesome, Maunsell got a brief phone call. He answered it, said 'Okay' and put the receiver down. He continued: 'Okay, that was Doug'. Shortly afterwards the threesome broke up. The third person with Maunsell and Gair was me.

When the story broke around Gair's head the next day, he grinned and said to milling journalists: 'I cannot comment. I'm not a politician any more. I'm a diplomat. I'll send you a shamrock from Dublin.'

In the upshot, the Gair Affair and the Night of the Long Prawns became irrelevant as manoeuvres in a half-Senate election because Opposition Leader Billy Snedden called for a double dissolution election, and in the Senate, the Coalition threatened to block Supply unless Whitlam brought one on. Unlike in November 1975, Whitlam accepted the double dissolution challenge and went to the people, with the seats of all Members of the House of Representatives and all Senators on the line.

It is well-recorded history that Labor won that 1974 election with a reduced majority of five in the House of Representatives, that it narrowly missed gaining control of the Senate, that the DLP was eliminated in the Senate, and that Snedden made a fool of himself by declaring: 'We were not defeated. We just did not win enough seats to form a government.' This statement set in train Malcolm Fraser's thrust for the overthrow of Snedden as Liberal leader. It also signalled the Coalition's renewed determination to still thwart Whitlam in the Senate.

The third and easily most significant controversy for the Whitlam Government was the Loans Affair. It had as its genesis a meeting of four Ministers in effective Executive Council at The Lodge: Whitlam, deputy Prime Minister and Treasurer Jim Cairns, Murphy, and Minerals and Energy Minister Rex Connor, who was known as 'the Strangler'. For reasons never fully explained, apart from Treasury antipathy and an apparent desire to avoid Loan Council scrutiny, they decided to go outside the usual Treasury channels to raise an extraordinarily big overseas loan of US$4000 million for Connor's ambitious development proposals.

Under the plan, the loan was to be for 20 years and for 'temporary purposes'. Government-run projects on which the money was to be spent included offshore oil, a national pipeline grid, and a coal liquefaction plant. This was a bizarre operation that was at best deeply misguided and at worst politically disastrous for Labor. It involved a strange Pakistani financier, Tirath Khemlani, who had never been heard of in conventional fund-raising channels such as the Union Bank of Switzerland, and who never delivered. The 'affair' led to: a special sitting of the House of Representatives; an attempt by the Coalition-dominated Senate to call leading public servants before it for investigation; a frantic Connor waiting by his telex machine for hours in the middle of the night for messages that never came from Khemlani; and allegations of 'funny money' by the Opposition.

It also confirmed the business community's fears that a spendthrift Whitlam Government, having pushed up salaries of the public service 'fat cats' and presided over inflation reaching almost 14 per cent, was out of control.

Further, it gave Malcolm Fraser the chance he wanted, 'the extraordinary and reprehensible circumstance' which on becoming Opposition Leader he had declared he was expecting so he could catch the Government 'with its pants down'. Much as Whitlam tried to prevent it, the Loans Affair consumed the Government for the first 10 months of 1975 and led to the Coalition's second blocking of Supply in the Senate.

Yet, ironically, the Loans Affair never resulted in a loan. Furthermore, the controversy never need have happened. If Whitlam and his colleagues had gone through the conventional channels of the Treasury and the Loan Council and insisted on some (more moderate) amount of money (whatever the Treasury opposition) for a start on Rex Connor's grandiose national development plans, there would have been no great negative headline-grabbing fuss.

To complement all this tumult there came sundry appointments and dismissals which were to have their adverse impact on Labor. There was Murphy's appointment to the High Court, at his request, which was immediately perceived as another 'job for the boys'. More importantly the Senate vacancy so created had to be filled—and the New South Wales Liberal Government ignored convention and filled it with a non-Labor Senator, one Cleaver Bunton of Albury.

Gough Whitlam demonstrates his classic penchant for ruins.

There was Lance Barnard's appointment, at his request, as Ambassador to Sweden, which led to the by-election in the Tasmanian seat of Bass in June 1975 and its loss by Labor in a 17 per cent swing, which in turn gave Fraser the impetus he needed.

There was Jim Cairns' appointment as Treasurer, at his request, in place of Frank Crean, and then Cairns' appointment of the woman of whom he had professed a 'love', Junie Morosi, as his personal assistant.

There was Whitlam's dismissal of Cairns for misleading the House over overseas loans, and Whitlam's dropping of Clyde Cameron, much against his wishes, from the Labor and Immigration portfolio. This was an act for which Cameron, always one of the great professional haters, never forgave him.

There was the sacking of Connor for misleading the Parliament over details of Khemlani's activities in the Loans Affair.

And as it was to turn out, surpassing all these, there was Gough Whitlam's personal choice and appointment of New South Wales Chief Justice Sir John Kerr as Governor-General. He was regarded by most of Whitlam's Ministers, particularly Senator 'Diamond Jim' McClelland, who had been a close court-room colleague of Kerr in earlier days, as a good choice. Nobody foresaw then the course that history, and Kerr, would take.

The dismissal of the Whitlam Government by Kerr was the most sensational single event in Australian political history. It has been well-documented, and written about by the chief protagonists—Kerr, Whitlam, Fraser, and the then Chief Justice of the High Court, Sir Garfield Barwick, from whom Kerr sought advice beforehand—and many others, and debated from all angles.

However, there are still some salient observations to be made. The Liberal-Country Party Coalition had the numbers in the Senate to block Supply (meaning the Appropriation Bills in the Budget which provide for the supply of money to all departments to fund government administration). But the Coalition only had this power because the New South Wales Liberal Government had broken convention with the appointment of Senator Bunton and because the Bjelke-Petersen Government in Queensland had broken convention with the appointment of non-Labor Senator Pat Field to fill a vacancy caused by the death of Labor Senator Bert Milliner.

Fraser, subsequently as Prime Minister, perhaps feeling a little conscience-stricken, was to ensure this disgraceful fiddling with casual Senate vacancies could not happen again. He promoted a referendum (one of only eight to succeed since Federation) to insert in the Constitution that such a 'casual' vacancy must be filled by a person from the same party that previously held the seat.

The Senate did, and still does, have the constitutional power to block Supply. Though it cannot initiate or amend money Bills under the Constitution, it can reject any Bill. Though Whitlam has made much retrospective play ever since about the inappropriateness, even impropriety, of the Senate blocking Supply—claiming that at stake was the authority of the House of Representatives as the national and democratic chamber—in Opposition previously both he and Murphy had threatened to do just that.

In August 1970, Whitlam said as Opposition Leader during debate on the 1970-71 Budget: 'Let me make it clear at the outset that our opposition to this Budget is no mere formality. We intend to press our opposition by all available means on all related measures in both Houses. If the motion is defeated, we will vote against the Bills here and in the Senate. Our purpose is to destroy this Budget and to destroy the Government which has sponsored it.'

If there is to be a solution to the Budget-blocking problem and if a repeat of the 1975 crisis is to be avoided, in my view the Constitution should be altered so that either the Senate does not have the power to reject Supply, or that power is retained and if Supply is blocked there will automatically be a double dissolution election, without the Governor-General having to adjudicate. The Governor-General did, and still does, have the reserve power to dismiss a government.

It was both disgraceful and sad that Kerr did not have

sufficient trust in his relationship with Whitlam—his chief adviser as Prime Minister—to feel able to discuss the unfolding Supply-blocking drama and its ramifications with him. It was just as unfortunate for Labor that an imperious Whitlam saw no need to do so. This lack of trust by the Whitlam-appointed Kerr led to an extraordinary trilogy of actions by a Governor-General: he refused to talk frankly with the Prime Minister, then decided to sack him, then conducted the dismissal as a tactical surprise.

Whitlam's tactical mistake, having been sacked by Kerr at 1.05 pm on 11 November 1975, was to concentrate only on how he would respond in the House. He forgot to tell or consult Ken Wreidt, Labor's leader in the Senate, which was where the blocking of Supply was taking place.

Kerr was correct in ordering an election so the people could decide. Kerr was not correct in keeping Fraser as (albeit caretaker) Prime Minister after the House of Representatives on the afternoon of 11 November, five times carried motions of no-confidence in Fraser and confidence in Whitlam. Supply having then been passed by the Opposition in the Senate and the processes for the 13 December double dissolution election being irrevocably in train, it should have been Whitlam and not Fraser who went into that election as Prime Minister.

In the electrifying atmosphere the campaign began immediately. Fraser and his team suddenly had all the administrative trappings of power and a stunned Labor Party had none.

There can be no doubt about the immense impact Whitlam had on the Labor Party, the Parliament and Australia. Domestically, he left his mark with a host of implemented policies: Medibank, the Schools Commission, the Technical and Further Education Commission, the abolition of students' tuition fees, and urban and regional development in particular. He especially liked Neville Wran's compliment: 'It was said of Caesar Augustus that he found a Rome of brick and left it of marble. It can be said of Gough Whitlam that he found Sydney, Melbourne and Brisbane unsewered and left them fully flushed.'

Whitlam welcomed the women's movement, supported the equal pay case, and placed the Office of the Status of Women under his direction. His Government established the Australia Council to promote the arts, and the Family Law Court. He initiated land rights to Aboriginals in the Northern Territory but backed away from pressing for them in the States.

The son of a distinguished public servant and consequently holding an impartial bureaucracy in high regard, Whitlam nevertheless started the politicisation of ministerial staffs with a deliberate expansion of personal advisers, often drawn from the bureaucratic ranks. This led to anger in sections of the public service, particularly the Treasury, and Whitlam had several clashes with Treasury Secretary Sir Frederick Wheeler. They were clashes in which Wheeler, who lived by the dictum that his role was to give 'frank and fearless advice', generally won the debate.

On one occasion when Whitlam threatened to sack him, Wheeler said the Prime Minister might note that he would probably have to abolish the Treasury itself. When Whitlam responded that he might just do that, Wheeler observed such a course would require a referendum because the Treasury was actually mentioned in the Constitution (Section 83).

On another occasion, when Whitlam ignored questions and observations from Wheeler about the likely illegality of the fund-raising methods in the Loans Affair and then told Wheeler he was on the skids, Wheeler retorted: 'Prime Minister, I wish to inform you of facts, your ignorance of which will bring you down.' History indeed indicates it was the prophetic Wheeler who had the last laugh.

When it came to the international stage, Whitlam was fond of describing himself, only a tad jokingly, as the best foreign minister Australia had produced. His diplomatic recognition of China by Australia was pertinent and overdue. His promotion of independence for Papua New Guinea was inevitable. He promoted a down-to-earth relationship with the USA.

His blind spot was a desire to view foreign relationships as tidy and centrist. Hence his tacit support for Indonesia when Suharto took over East Timor after it claimed independence from Portugal, and his de jure recognition of Soviet sovereignty over the Baltic States.

His penchant for overseas travel also added to his undoing, not least during the summer of 1974 when he interrupted an extensive tour in Europe to but briefly visit Darwin in the aftermath of Cyclone Tracy and then flew back to Europe again. Fraser made much play of calling him the 'tourist Prime Minister'.

However, the Whitlam Government's most serious faults lay in economic management. Though he has been unjustly criticised for lowering tariffs by 25 per cent across the board (and note, he was praised by business at the time and nobody ever raised them again afterwards), his government presided over an unprecedented wages-push inflationary explosion.

His Government deliberately used the Commonwealth Public Service as a pacesetter for wages. At the same time there was considerable militant adventurism by unions affiliated with the Labor Party. Much of the blame can be attributed to the fact that Bob Hawke wore two hats: that of ACTU president and that of ALP federal president. It can also be attributed to a poor relationship and a sense of rivalry between Hawke and Whitlam. This was more than a problem of communication between a Labor Government and the union movement.

In the final analysis, once the 1975 election campaign was under way, most voters forgot about the circumstances of Whitlam's dismissal and voted in accordance with their hip pocket nerves. The Coalition had beaten him in the Parliament with the help of Kerr's ambush but it was the perceived state of the economy which broke him at the ballot boxes.

Despite Whitlam's charisma, his call for his followers to 'maintain the rage', and big enthusiastic public rallies, opinion polls made it clear Labor was in for a drubbing. Fraser campaigned successfully on economic issues, even though the Budget the Coalition had blocked, the one produced by Treasurer Bill Hayden, had been a tight one, aimed at recovery from earlier excesses.

Whitlam suffered the biggest defeat ever meted out in an election—91 seats to 36, which meant there was a Coalition majority of 55. The Liberal Party had a majority in its own right. The crash-through-or-crash man had finally crashed.

In Queensland, once an electoral stamping ground favoured by Whitlam, every seat but Hayden's seat of Oxley was won by the Liberal or National parties. Hayden, who had received 68.9 per cent of the vote in 1972, narrowly escaped having to go to preferences with 50.2 per cent of the vote in 1975.

However, Whitlam did not resign immediately from Parliament. He was re-endorsed as Labor leader by the depleted caucus, and survived a mid-term challenge from Hayden by two votes. He even weathered the dreadful embarrassment of revelations (by Laurie Oakes) in 1976 that in the 1975 campaign he had been involved in weird Labor Party negotiations (along with Victorian Left-winger

Bill Hartley and ALP federal secretary David Combe) for a $500 000 contribution from the Iraqi Government towards election expenses.

As in the case of the Loans Affair, the Whitlam Government never did get the money. But Kim Beazley Snr, the most ethical of politicians, resigned from the shadow Cabinet in protest against Whitlam's participation in the affair. Finally in the 1977 elections, called early by Fraser, Labor again suffered heavy defeat—86 seats to 38, a Coalition majority of 48—and Whitlam departed the parliamentary scene.

He had been astride the stage. To that point (Hawke later was to better his feat) he had been the only Labor leader to win two consecutive elections, in 1972 and 1974. He also had led Labor to its two biggest defeats, in 1975 and 1977.

He had been Prime Minister for less than three years, and he carried on for the next 27 years as if he had never left The Lodge. He continued to entertain and lecture the party faithful. He drew acclamation at every venue. The Hawke Government made him Ambassador to UNESCO, based in Paris. He continued to indulge his classical passion and knowledge by leading selected tours of Australians on overseas visits to antiquities. He became a distinguished chairman of the National Gallery of Australia.

Two years into the 21st century he was, at 86, still making a remarkable professional living as Emeritus Prime Minister. He went to China in 2002 to accept accolades on the 30th anniversary of the opening up of diplomatic relations. He was still adored by his fans and increasingly respected by most of his former enemies.

Innocents in a Vietnam mine field! Anzac Day 1966, these correspondents accompanied Prime Minister Harold Holt to the Bien Hoa airstrip near Saigon. Army public relations officer, Captain Ken Blanch, is third from the left. Brown is squatting in front, third from the right.

Twenty-five years later, on 26 April 1991, Blanch wrote a revealing article in *The Courier-Mail*:

'I feel again the cold sweat of that prime ministerial visit', he said, 'when a US helicopter pilot, misreading the coloured smoke I had put up for him, lands a helicopter loaded with the cream of Australian journalism in a minefield fenced off and abandoned after the French Indochina war a decade before.'

Man in the middle of a 'sweetheart agreement' between former arch foes Prime Minister Gough Whitlam (right) and Queensland Premier Sir Joh Bjelke-Petersen is Brown. On 14 February, 1975, Whitlam's sense of humour led him to ask Brown to his office to witness their signatures on a Commonwealth-Queensland sewerage agreement. 'It's St. Valentine's Day', Whitlam quipped, 'and this is a sweetheart agreement. You are the appropriate person to witness these historic documents.'

Overlooking North Korea, Prime Minister Malcolm Fraser, an avid photographer, prepares his camera alongside a South Korean sentry tower at Panmunjon in the Demilitarised Zone, May 1982. For Brown (behind, left) the most enduring memory of the Demilitarised Zone, 210 km long and 4 km wide, is the re-vegetation and the profusion of birds, especially cranes and pheasants, in a corridor of no-mans-land across the Korean Peninsular, which has had no people in it for half a century.

Television journalist Kenn Begg (left) and Wallace Brown, relax in the Prime Ministerial RAAF Boeing 707 on an overseas trip. On this occasion in 1984, Bob Hawke was PM and the party was returning from Kuala Lumpur to Canberra at the end of a trip, which also took in Japan, South Korea and China. The media organisations represented by the accompanying journalists pay the full business class airfare to the RAAF to travel in the Prime Minister's aircraft.

Fraser

NOT MEANT TO BE EASY

**John Malcolm Fraser, Liberal (1975–1983)
7 years, 4 months.**

'Life is not meant to be easy my child, but take courage, it can be delightful.'
George Bernard Shaw, in Back to Methuselah, *which Fraser originally quoted in full, and from which the condensed version was drawn.*

'If I were producing a play......I could make a stage success of him as a 16th century cardinal but not a 20th century prime minister.'
Paul Hasluck, in The Chance of Politics

When the 45-year-old Malcolm Fraser waited, literally, in the wings at Government House, Yarralumla, at 12.55 pm on 11 November 1975, for Sir John Kerr to sack Gough Whitlam, he knew with rolled-gold certainty he would be Prime Minister in 10 minutes time.

No person has become Prime Minister of Australia (albeit officially a 'caretaker' one for a short period) in more controversial circumstances, and knowledge of that was to weigh forever upon him. This was despite the fact he had engineered those circumstances and despite his confirmation in office, with the largest majority in Australian history, by voters at the subsequent general election on 13 December.

Yet no Prime Minister had already revelled in controversy as much, even deliberately shaped major crises, as Fraser. No Prime Minister was more complex, projecting a persona of apparent contradictions. Few politicians have been more formidable. Fraser, never able to easily make friends and consequently never apparently averse to making enemies, had already left a trail of casualties behind him. In four years he had destroyed a Liberal Prime Minister, a Liberal Opposition Leader and a Labor Prime Minister.

Having participated in the making of John Gorton in late 1967, he had precipitated the crisis that led to Gorton's unmaking in 1971 with the charge he was not fit to hold office. Having failed at one attempt to depose Billy Snedden as Liberal Opposition leader, he had succeeded at the second bid, on 21 March 1975, by 37 votes to 27 in a party room ballot. It was at a press conference immediately afterwards that he had announced his aim was to catch Whitlam with his pants down.

As the 1975 political-cum-pseudo constitutional crisis developed with the Coalition's insistence on blocking

Supply in the Senate, it fell to Steele Hall—the former small-l liberal Liberal Premier of South Australia who ended the conservative establishment Liberal Party's gerrymander, then formed the breakaway Liberal Movement and became a Senator and later re-joined the Liberal Party and won a House of Representatives seat—to make the most prescient of comments.

Winning IS everything for Fraser, as it is for Ian Chappell. (Refers to the incident in which Ian Chappell ordered his brother, Greg, to bowl under-arm in a match against New Zealand).

Hall, then a Liberal Movement Senator, did so in a letter to Fraser, then Opposition Leader, on 1 October 1975. A steadfast opponent of Fraser's tactic to block Supply in the Senate and force an early election, Hall said, in part: 'I believe Labor will be defeated whenever a general election is held. In this event it is very important that the manner in which you assume office should have the long-term approval of most Australians.'

Hall also wrote: 'It is to our advantage (on the non-Labor

side of politics) therefore, that the conventions should be observed. I suggest you are the only person who has the authority to restore them. A clear statement from you that the (Labor) Government will live or die by its numbers in the House of Representatives would be adequate for the purpose.'

Malcolm Fraser, of course, never gave such an undertaking, and ever afterwards had to accept the consequences of his means of coming to office. Though the public anger of many electors was directed at the increasingly sorry figure of Kerr (and particularly after Fraser appointed him as Ambassador to UNESCO in Paris in a failed bid to take the heat off him as an issue), Fraser was ever conscious that many people would never forgive him either. He had a great habit of saying in private conversation he had simply done what was 'right'. But it was a defensive habit.

His complex nature could be seen in several ways. On the one hand he developed a desire to bandage the wounds. He had the good sense to make Sir Zelman Cowen Governor-General in succession to Kerr, because Cowen, one of Australia's greatest constitutional lawyers, was a healer. Fraser kept the Whitlam-appointed John Menadue on as Secretary of the Prime Minister's Department, and later made him Ambassador to Japan.

Fraser also knew the social and democratic fabric of Australia might indeed be ripped if State governments ever again flouted convention and appointed 'casual' senators of different political persuasion (as the Queensland and New South Wales non-Labor governments had done in 1975) to that of those they were replacing. As a result he promoted the referendum change to the Constitution which now makes it mandatory for casual Senate vacancies to be filled by senators of similar political allegiance. What used to be mere convention became a constitutional requirement.

At the same time, Fraser, who had once been the great

risk-taker, and an exponent of brinkmanship, was never quite game as Prime Minister to use a rare government majority in the Senate to push through necessary economic reforms. Having used Coalition numbers in the Senate with such devastating effect in 1975 when he was in Opposition, he never did so when he was in office. Having often failed to consult colleagues when in Opposition, he never learnt how to delegate administrative responsibility. His capacity for work and long hours was legendary. But he spent so much time consulting people in government at any hour of the day and night that he was often bogged down in detail. Yet on some key issues, albeit ones in which he had sole prime ministerial prerogative such as appointing a Governor-General or deciding on an election date, he consulted very few people if anybody.

On his departure from Parliament he described his greatest achievement as 'economic realism'. In fact, his government engaged in economic tardiness. The emerging market-forces-type 'dries' of the Liberal Party never really forgave him for baulking at Treasurer John Howard's early attempts at labour market and tax reforms. Corporate tax evasion was but ineffectively tackled.

As a Victorian grazier Malcolm Fraser was more in tune ideologically with key National Party figures such as Doug Anthony, Ian Sinclair and Peter Nixon than with the reformists, who would privately (but never publicly while he was Prime Minister) describe him as 'another agrarian socialist'.

Fraser spoke about the need for competition but kept the two-airline duopoly because the National Party feared a fall-off in services to the bush. His Cabinet 'razor-gang' did not really slice dramatically into public service excesses and duplications. He even became a softie when he constantly backed Social Security Minister Dame Margaret Guilfoyle in Cabinet when spending on welfare went way over Budget.

Malcolm Fraser writes his memoirs in 1987. John Howard is underwhelmed.

However, he did try seriously to get Commonwealth-States financial relations on a better footing by legislating to allow the States to raise some of their own income tax with a special levy (but was beaten by the parochial States throwing up their hands in hypocritical mock shock and horror). His rhetoric and patrician image were often harsher than his actions.

On the other hand, Fraser remained a confrontationist by nature. He simply did not try to soften that image, nor the inaccurate one of ultra-conservatism which his opponents painted.

One of the great ironies of Fraser's career is he inadvertently was responsible for the formation of the Australian Democrats by former Liberal Don Chipp. If he had kept Chipp, who had been a shadow minister in Opposition, in his team as a Minister when the Coalition won government,

Chipp never would have resigned from the Liberal Party and formed the Democrats to 'keep the bastards honest'.

Like Whitlam, Fraser was tall (6 foot 5 inches or 195 centimetres) and had a physical presence. Unlike Whitlam he was shy, uneasy with people he did not know, and not a gifted speaker. Charismatic he was not. He hid his unease by being aloof, aggressive and argumentative. It was *Sydney Morning Herald* journalist Peter Bowers who first likened Fraser's stern facial features to those of an Easter Island statue. He did not have a subtle sense of humour like Whitlam, and some of his colleagues used to complain about his party trick of putting melting ice cubes surreptitiously in their pockets.

Yet Fraser could also be genuinely and superbly hospitable as the country gentleman, a facet of his character which few people saw. One of the advantages for a journalist who has been around some time in the hothouse of Canberra Town is that you 'grow up' with young people—politicians and bureaucrats in particular—who later move into positions of considerable importance. So it was with Malcolm Fraser, who spent much of his time living in Canberra in the 1960s as a backbencher with his wife Tammy and young children. Our two families socialised on an irregular basis. Tammy was a splendid foil for him, and became one of the more successful and charming prime ministerial wives.

Subsequently, when he was Prime Minister, Fraser was presiding over a federal Cabinet meeting in Adelaide, which was to have ended on a Friday afternoon so everybody, journalists included, could get home for the weekend. However, by 7 pm that Friday, with most commercial aircraft having already left Adelaide, it was clear the Cabinet business was not finished and so Fraser decided the meeting would resume on the Sunday afternoon.

He was going home to his Victorian Western Districts property, Nareen, by chartered light aircraft, for most of the weekend, while everyone else was cursing him for disrupting their personal plans. As he walked out the door of an anteroom in the hotel where the Cabinet was meeting he said to me: 'What are you doing for the weekend?' I replied: 'I'll stay in Adelaide I guess'. Said Fraser: 'Well I'm going home to Nareen. I've got the annual bull sales on. Want to come?'

I went in the light aircraft and was treated to Malcolm and Tammy's bush hospitality. My attempt at trout-fishing in one of their dams was amateurish and the bull sales went without incident. Politics were discussed at length and with considerable passion over several meals with relations and neighbours. The conversation covered Bjelke-Petersen's political longevity and Fraser criticised the Queensland electoral gerrymander. He complained about the Premiers who had rejected his income tax surcharge proposal. We inspected his cellar. It was a memorable weekend.

It would be a mistake to think Malcolm Fraser's seven years of administrative power resulted in nothing much. He had many positive achievements, which give the lie to recent observations by people surprised about how much he has changed, how much more liberal, socialist even, he has become since he has left office. The basic fact is, he has not changed. The 'new' Malcolm is the old Fraser. The tradition of noblesse oblige ran in his family. The only real difference is that in his later and mellower years he has bothered to explain.

On rights for Aboriginals, for instance, it was Fraser who extended native land title rights in the States, much against the wishes of the governments of Queensland and Western Australia in particular. It was Fraser who appointed three particularly sensitive liberal Aboriginal Affairs Ministers: Fred Chaney, Ian Viner and Peter Baume who, for example, used federal powers to establish Aboriginal councils and associations. It was Fraser, largely influenced by Greek-born staffer Petro Georgiou of Melbourne (and later Andrew Peacock's successor as the Liberal MP for Kooyong), who boosted multiculturalism. When it came to race he was always colour-blind.

Overseas, it was Fraser as Prime Minister who strongly supported black Africans in Zimbabwe and South Africa. It was Fraser who took an anti-Thatcher stand at the 1977 Commonwealth Heads of Government Conference in London on the need for Rhodesia to become an independent Zimbabwe and it was Fraser who supported the Gleneagles Agreement to sever sporting links with South Africa for as long as it adhered to apartheid (unlike John Howard, who always opposed sanctions against South Africa).

It was Fraser who sacked Queensland National Party Senator Glen Sheil as a minister before Sheil had even been sworn in. This was because Sheil had made pro-apartheid comments to an enterprising young Press Gallery journalist Niki Savva in an interview when his appointment was announced. It was Fraser who deliberately mixed politics with sport when he banned from touring Australia those members of a West Indian cricket team who had played in South Africa.

It was Fraser who backed US President Jimmy Carter's protest against the Soviet invasion of Afghanistan to such an extent that he tried to stop Australia from participating in the Moscow Olympics. He was beaten however, by a rather more popular and anti-establishment Fraser, first name Dawn, no relation, who ran a high-profile 'swim for Australia' campaign.

It was Fraser who supported developing Third World countries in their bid to get better treatment from developed industrial nations, in what became known interminably as the North-South Dialogue. It was the Fraser Government, with Ian McPhee as Immigration Minister, which accepted and organised an orderly inflow of about 100 000 Indochinese refugees in the late 1970s.

On the environment, it was Fraser who used the Federal Government's external powers (which give it control over exports) to stop sand-mining on Fraser Island, much to the anger of Queensland Premier Bjelke-Petersen and other fervent States-rightists on the non-Labor side of politics. (But Fraser baulked when it came to standing up to the Liberal States-rightists of Tasmania and using Commonwealth powers to stop the building of the Franklin Dam—an approach which his successor Bob Hawke did not hesitate to take.) It also was Fraser who eventually listened to the anti-whaling lobby Project Jonah in 1977, and to his daughter Phoebe, and ignored the advice of his own department and Primary Industry Minister Ian Sinclair, and led the fight to ban whaling.

And in the Torres Strait, it was Fraser who eventually succeeded where Gough Whitlam had failed. He negotiated a practical border zone arrangement between Australia and Papua New Guinea. His success in the Torres Strait can be attributed to three factors: his innate stubbornness, his willingness to stay put on an island in the strait until the basis for a solution was reached, and his refusal to accept defeat. This is Fraser's most understated single achievement.

Solution to the border issue was long overdue. Whitlam's proposal, that the border be re-aligned to about the middle of Torres Strait while Australia was still the legal power on both sides of it, had been superbly logical in principle. Yet it was impractical in implementation because it did not allow for the fact that Torres Strait Islanders and coastal Papuans were often interrelated and simply plied their boats and their wares to and forth all the time, always had done and always would do.

Nor had Whitlam allowed for the populism and demagoguery of Bjelke-Petersen, who waged a successful pro-Queensland, concede-not-an-inch, and anti-Canberra campaign.

Fraser, however, took both these problems into account. Unlike Whitlam he went to the Torres Strait, was hailed ceremonially as the first Prime Minister to do so, had the lighthouse tender Cape Moreton on station as his accommodation and command-and-communications headquarters, and prepared to stay there. He assembled on Yam Island, initially sitting in the sand in a circle under its ceremonial 'wisdom tree', all the necessary stakeholders: islander leaders including the influential George Mye, representatives of local coastal Papuans, the Queensland Government and the Papua New Guinea Government, Foreign Minister Andrew Peacock and the federal National Party MP for Leichhardt, David Thomson.

After what seemed interminable and tense talks in the heat and the sand, a patient and stubborn Fraser got what he wanted. There was general consensus in which the islanders accepted that the Commonwealth Government and not Bjelke-Petersen was their spokesman, and an arrangement whereby there should be a protected border 'zone' for both the islanders and the coastal Papuans. Though the international territorial boundary which takes Australian sovereignty to within sight of the Papuan mainland would remain, the special zone, covering most of the Torres Strait, was accepted by all parties as a solution. This was later formally agreed upon by Michael Somare and Peacock in Port Moresby.

Fraser displayed the same sort of can-do stubbornness on a bigger international stage, when he went to Brussels in 1977. He forced the smooth sophisticated bureaucrats of the European Commission to negotiate an agreement, and sign a piece of paper at the last moment, on steel imports from Australia—when all they wanted to do was talk pleasantries over lunch and dinner.

For the more iconoclastic members of the Press Gallery, the stolid Malcolm Fraser ironically was often a lot of fun. Travelling overseas with him provided some unforgettable moments. Possibly the most significant of these occurred at the White House, because it was a timely reminder that though the USA, inevitably, is very big in any Australian Government's eyes, the reverse does not apply.

On his first official visit to Washington as Prime Minister, Fraser was given the full-on ceremonial treatment by President Carter—complete with trumpets, cannon, red carpet on the steps leading to the South Lawn and guard of honour of Marines. The two stood on the dais, with Fraser basking in the glory of the occasion as he shared a platform with the most powerful man on earth. He was not the first or last Prime Minister to be caught up in the gravitas of such an event.

In all this hype and circumstance, Carter advanced to his microphone and intoned gravely: 'And now I welcome to the United States of America, the Prime Minister of our great ally Australia, my great and good friend... John!' For the mickey-taking Australian press this was hilarious, but it also had a serious twist. It is a pity the US President had not been a little better briefed so that he knew to call Fraser by his middle name and not by his first name.

However, the Americans made amends on a subsequent visit in 1981, or at least the University of South Carolina (USC) did, when it conferred on him an honorary Doctorate of Laws. Indeed the USC went over the top and Malcolm Fraser knew God was on his side. The reason for the accolade was never entirely clear. Some of his advisers wondered politely why we were going to South Carolina in the first place, and some of the dozens of US security men wondered who it was they had been assigned to protect. However, the university did make a big play with its International Studies Institute.

Came the colourful ceremony and the deep southern adulation began in the invocation by university chaplain Dr Donald Jones. His arms were lifted to the heavens: 'Lord God', he intoned magnificently, 'who doth raise up leaders among nations, we acknowledge thy wisdom in setting apart the Australian Prime Minister Malcolm Fraser.' Phlegmatic Australians in the Fraser party blinked a little as the chaplain continued: 'Thou has endowed him with the qualities extended to his office and thou dost walk with him both among his own people and throughout the international community.' 'Lord God', called the chaplain, 'we thank thee for giving us, and the world... John... Malcolm... Fraser.' All of which the recipient of this praise thought was pretty fitting stuff, and after a standing ovation at a dinner that followed, Fraser almost cracked a wide grin when he said: 'If any of you wish to come to Australia at any time to campaign on my behalf you will be more than welcome.'

Two particular offbeat events occurred in China, which Fraser, following in the footsteps of Whitlam, visited in 1976, and which, like Whitlam, he embraced. He and his party were given the right royal orchestrated treatment, from daily banquets to hordes of flag-waving dancing girls. Ironically this was partly because of his hard-line attitude against the Soviet Union, with which China had fallen out at that time.

On an escorted tour along the Great Wall of China, he removed his shoes so he would not slip, and so was walking up one of the steep slopes in his socks. He was suddenly told by an aide that *The* (Melbourne) *Herald* that afternoon was running a story by Peter Costigan (Lord Mayor of Melbourne a quarter-century later) about him proposing a four-power alliance between Australia, the USA, Japan and China. Anxious to refute this while he had all the Australian media representatives beside him, he immediately announced he was having a press briefing—and away he launched into a detailed analysis of Australian defence and foreign policy.

At the same time, however, Tammy Fraser gave a small involuntary shriek. She had been cleaning a contact lens with a tissue and dropped it. She started to scrabble around in the dust. Consequently, while some members of the party listened dutifully to Fraser, others fell to their knees to help Mrs Fraser find the contact lens (which they eventually did).

It was clear that our Chinese hosts, including the chief of protocol, were rather bemused at the sight of a shoeless Australian Prime Minister talking at great length about Australian foreign policy on the Great Wall while his wife and media people who were supposed to be listening to him were rummaging at his feet in the dust. John Menadue, accompanying Fraser as Secretary of the Prime Minister's Department, said: 'All this rabble needs now to complete the picture are Mongolian hordes coming over the horizon.'

A few days later the Fraser party was in remote Urumchi, in the far north-west of Sinkiang province, west of the Gobi Desert and the most distant city from the open sea in the world. The welcoming celebrations were immense. Fraser may have been the first foreign leader to have visited the place since Marco Polo trod the old Silk Road. If not, he was certainly treated as such, and we Caucasians were objects of such curiosity that thousands of people lined the streets just to stare and touch.

On the second night there was a lavish banquet given by the local Uigur councillors, headed by the Mayor. It lasted for many hours and many toasts of mao-tai, possibly the most potent little alcoholic drink ever distilled. As the banquet neared its end in the small hours, the Mayor called for yet another toast and the local dignitaries sang their 'national' (meaning Sinkiang) anthem, making it clear this was not the all-China anthem as decreed by the bothersome far-away authorities in Beijing. Not to be outdone, Fraser responded and said the Australian party would sing Australia's national anthem.

'Yes, yes', came the enthusiastic voice of ABC television reporter Ken Begg, 'Australia's national anthem!', and before Fraser could launch into 'Advance Australia Fair', Begg was leading the Australian media contingent in a rousing rendition of... 'We like Aeroplane Jelly!'

Fraser glared as only he could. He was not amused. But he could do nothing. 'Aeroplane Jelly' was carried through to its finish. Tammy laughed loudly and other Australian officials joined in. The Mayor advanced on Tammy and insisted on dancing with her. The Mayor then congratulated the Prime Minister on (according to the interpreter) the 'lovely lilt of Australia's national anthem'. Fraser smiled the barest of flinty smiles and held his tongue. He did not confuse things by trying to explain. Nor did he bother to rebuke Begg. It is possible that to this day the Uigurs of Urumchi think 'Aeroplane Jelly' is our national anthem.

Another incident also involved Begg. On a visit to Mexico City to promote the virtues of the need for developing nations to be helped by becoming engaged in the North-South Dialogue, Malcolm Fraser made a speech about his mission. His halting monotone always was hard to listen to even when he was on the liveliest of subjects. On this occasion everything he said had to be interpreted and many members of his audience were nodding off. Begg sent back a report to Australian television viewers that Fraser, in expounding on his most worthy subject, had given an 'eye-glazing speech' which highlighted the difficulty of him getting his message across.

The next day, when summaries of the Australian media reports were telexed back to him from Australia, Malcolm Fraser was angry. He called us in for a special briefing, making the point that he expected more cooperation from the Australian press and stressing that he was not engaged in an 'eye-glazing' operation. He was so worked up about the phrase that he then went into a joint media conference with the Mexican President and twice said that though some commentators thought his mission was 'eye-glazing' this was not so.

His remarks were duly interpreted for the benefit of Mexican journalists and I noticed that each time he said 'eye-glazing' the Mexicans hesitated before writing in their notepads. I asked the interpreter how he had translated 'eye-glazing'. He replied: 'The closest I could get was "vision-stopping".'

I passed this on to Begg, who could not resist the temptation to use it. He sent his next report back to Australia that Fraser, in furthering his commendable cause about North-South Dialogue, had told the Mexicans there was nothing 'vision-stopping' about it. It was an incident which reminded the official Australian party that the Australian media representatives did not see themselves as servants of the government.

A feature of any style of government is eventual ministerial change, but in Fraser's case it came too often. This developed into a picture of instability, of an autocratic Prime Minister who did not interact well with his Ministers. He was also known to announce what he described as a 'government decision' before it had been taken. Though this preempted opposition within his Cabinet, it upset many Ministers.

On one occasion I was talking to Defence Minister Jim

Killen in his office after a Cabinet meeting when a staffer entered and said the Prime Minister had just announced that the Government had decided to give some patrol boats to Indonesia. Said a startled Killen: 'But we have not decided that, not yet anyway. There are some loose ends.' He called Doug Anthony, who was equally surprised, but who reacted with equanimity: 'Well, Jim, I guess we've decided now. We will just have to wear it.'

The Fraser Government saw constant changes. One Cabinet Minster, Ivor Greenwood, died. Four, including Liberal elder Robert Cotton, were given overseas diplomatic posts. Former Attorney-General Robert Ellicott, regarded by lawyers in the Parliament as possessor of one of the great legal minds, chose to leave because of frustration. Treasurer Phillip Lynch was stood down during the 1977-election campaign because of allegations he had used his position to benefit from property deals. In the upshot, Fraser won the election easily, and Lynch was cleared and remained as deputy Liberal leader. In 1982, Lynch left Parliament because of terminal illness.

There were other instances of change: Western Australian Reg Withers—known as 'the Toecutter' for his commanding and unflappable role as Opposition Leader in the Senate during the 1974 and 1975 Budget-blocking exercises—was dismissed by Fraser for the ridiculous reason that as Administrative Affairs Minister responsible for the Electoral Commission he had suggested a name change (but not at any time a boundary change) to a Queensland electorate.

A Royal Commission had found (wrongly in my view) that Withers had acted with 'impropriety', but said he had not tried to influence the Electoral Commissioners in the redistribution. Fraser insisted that Withers go. It was a totally unnecessary act by Fraser in the name of 'propriety, the right thing to do'. The only practical result was to alienate Withers, who had been his master tactician in the Senate, but who then became a rebellious Andrew Peacock's de facto campaign manager.

The changes continued. Two Ministers, Michael MacKellar and John Moore, were told to resign by Fraser after MacKellar brought a colour television set through Customs without paying duty. One Minister, Queenslander Eric Robinson, refused to serve when he was demoted to the outer ministry. Ian Sinclair stood down after being charged with forgery in a NSW court. He was found not guilty and reinstated but the impression of instability grew.

Most destabilising of all was the resignation of Peacock from the Ministry in April 1981. This was essentially a personality clash, clothed in principles about policy towards Cambodia by Peacock. Peacock quoted, word for word, the 'disloyalty' charges Fraser had used against Gorton a decade earlier. Fraser took him on, needling him over several months into a direct challenge for the leadership in 1982. Fraser won easily. Six months later, after Tony Eggleton intervened on his behalf, Peacock was back in the Ministry, but the damage had been done in the perception of the public.

The image was projected of an increasingly confrontationist Prime Minister who was fighting the States, the unions and business all at the same time, and who was leading a shifting and unstable government.

At the same time, Bill Hayden, who had succeeded Whitlam as Opposition Leader, had revamped the Labor Party as a well-organised and genuine alternative government, with shadow ministers who were well-versed in their responsibilities and increasingly able to confront Fraser's Ministers on their own turf. And Bob Hawke was in Parliament and starting to make his run. He had failed in a first attempt to overthrow Hayden, but was moving towards a second.

Along came one of the most significant by-elections in

Australian history, in the Victorian seat of Flinders in December 1982, following the resignation of Lynch. In importance it rivalled the by-elections in Dawson in 1966 and Bass in 1975. The Liberals retained Flinders (the new member being Peter Reith) but pointedly there was a swing to Labor of 3 per cent. This affected judgements on both sides of politics. On the Liberal side, Fraser decided to ignore the swing to Labor and reckoned he could win an early general election. On the Labor side, Hawke and his supporters reckoned that if Hayden could not achieve better than a 3 per cent swing, it was time to replace him.

Realising this, Fraser remained anxious to bring on an early election, in an attempt to catch Labor while it was rumbling about who would be leader. He was about to do so late in 1982 when his back gave way and he was forced to go to bed. Early in 1983 he was still hell-bent on an election. But he left it too late. On 3 February he made his move.

It was the biggest mistake he ever made. When he went out to Yarralumla at noon to advise Governor-General Sir Ninian Stephen he wanted a double dissolution election, Hayden was Labor Leader. But the Governor-General was hosting a lunch for a departing Polish ambassador and said he could not read Fraser's formal request and advice until after that. At 1.30 pm Hayden announced he was resigning as Labor leader. A cautious Ninian Stephen read Fraser's letter and asked for one point to be clarified, and by the time he formally agreed to Fraser's election request, at 4.30 pm, Hawke was Labor Leader.

Far from there being serious and drawn-out public in-fighting between Hayden and Hawke supporters leading up to a Labor caucus meeting, as Fraser had expected, Hawke had walked into the job in a quick bloodless coup conducted in a meeting of the federal parliamentary Labor Party executive in Brisbane. Hayden, under heavy pressure from frontbenchers who deserted him, walked the plank unhappily but without resistance, muttering at a press conference that a 'drover's dog' could win the election for Labor under the circumstances. He did so for the good of the party which was now in an election campaign. He also knew that to do anything else would be futile.

In Canberra, Fraser declared it made no difference. With considerable bravado he said: 'It will be the first election in which two Labor leaders were knocked off in one go.' Everyone at the press conference saw this for the bluster it was. Hawke, at that time the most popular person in Australia according to all opinion polls, campaigned on virtually the single issue of national reconciliation. He won comfortably with a majority of 25 against the great confrontationist when the election was held on 3 March.

Malcolm Fraser's stern visage twisted and he shed a tear as he conceded defeat at a Melbourne hotel, congratulating Hawke and accepting sole responsibility for the timing and conduct of the election. Realising the division he would continue to cause within the Liberal Party, Fraser had the sense to resign from Parliament. He said: 'My decision to leave has not been taken because I want to be out of Parliament.' He walked out at the age of 52.

He spent the remaining 17 years of the 20th century seeking legitimacy in a worthy life-after-politics. He failed in a bid to become Secretary-General of the Commonwealth. He was an Eminent Person appointed by Hawke to help bring an end to apartheid in South Africa. He was the head of the Care Australia aid agency. He was a newspaper columnist espousing generally liberal, republican, pro-Aboriginal, nationalist and anti-pure market forces views.

In 2001 and 2002, as the Howard Government flung asylum seekers into detention camps for long periods, Fraser spoke out increasingly against it, labelling Australia's treatment of refugees as 'shameful'. Of the four living former prime ministers in mid-2002—the others being Whitlam, Hawke and Keating, all Labor men—he was the only one consistently to do so.

By then, many liberal/social commentators, who had criticised him savagely when he was in office, were seeing him in a welcome liberal light. He attained legitimacy. He repeatedly angered the Howard Government. He never lost his critics in the conservative rightist corner of the Liberal Party.

In September of 2002, Fraser joined Hayden, Whitlam and Hawke (and three former services chiefs and the president of the Returned Services League) in opposing any commitment of Australian forces in support of a US military offensive against Iraq without the backing of a specific United Nations' Security Council resolution.

Hawke

G'DAY, MATE

Robert James Lee Hawke, Labor (1983–1990)
8 years, 9 months and 8 days.

'In most people, there is, I believe, ultimately a desire for harmony rather than conflict.'

Hawke in his 1979 Boyer lectures on
the resolution of conflict

'By 1990 no Australian child will be living in poverty.'

Hawke in 1987 election policy speech

Bob Hawke, Rhodes Scholar, former Australian Council of Trade Unions president, lawyer, former Australian Labor Party president, former Reserve Bank Board member, was the son of a Congregational minister and the holder of the world's beer-drinking record.

An extrovert in marked contrast to the seemingly aloof Malcolm Fraser, he came to the leadership of the Labor Party denying he had blood on his hands. He said this, angrily, in an ABC television interview with Richard Carleton which more than anything else, revealed the arrogance of both men.

Thirty days later, having never sat in the House of Representatives as Opposition Leader, Hawke came to prime ministerial office projecting a grand aura of national reconciliation and economic summitry. From the very beginning he had no self-doubts.

His campaign slogan, 'Bringing Australia Together', was as banal as most others dreamt up by strategists of all parties, but it was considerably more intelligent than the Liberals' 'We are not waiting for the world'. He also had one great advantage over the tiring Malcolm Fraser: he was fighting an election campaign while still in his honeymoon period as Labor leader. Public opinion polls repeatedly indicated he was immensely popular, with a personal rating as high as 75 per cent.

Thanks to Hayden, who had resigned with good grace and heavy heart at that crucial meeting of Labor's parliamentary executive in Brisbane—and to Lionel Bowen and John Button, who had persuaded Hayden to depart peacefully—Hawke had become leader without having to engage in a traditional public Labor slugfest.

So it was that he felt supremely confident at his first post-coup press conference on 8 February 1983, when he referred to 'my Ministers'. He outlined his manifesto in presidential style, and declared, almost with the panache of Whitlam 11 years earlier: 'We are taking over government. We are ready for it.'

Indeed Labor was. Its campaign, directed by national secretary Bob McMullan, was efficient. In contrast to the Liberals and Fraser, who had been caught off-guard, the ALP and Hawke ran a virtually flawless operation. Even down to the Hawke riposte (supplied by lobbyist and consultant Richard Farmer), to Fraser's claim that the only thing people could do with their money to keep it safe under Labor would be to hoard it: 'But they can't put their savings under the bed, because that's where the Commies are!'

The election outcome was never really in doubt and when the numbers went up in the tally room on 5 March, Labor had a sweeping victory and a majority of 25 in the House of Representatives. Hawke was Australia's 23rd Prime Minister at the age of 54. It had been a spectacular ascendancy and it was to be the first of several prime ministerial milestones for Hawke as he re-wrote the record books.

He went on to win three more consecutive elections (against Andrew Peacock in 1984, John Howard in 1987, and Peacock again in 1990), and lost none. It was a feat never achieved by a Labor leader before and only beaten by Menzies (and equalled by Fraser and Howard). Early in 1987 Hawke passed the term of three years, eight months and 29 days set by his hero John Curtin to become the longest-serving Labor Prime Minister. In 1990 he passed Malcolm Fraser's term of seven years and four months to become the second-longest serving Prime Minister after Menzies.

Like Menzies, Hawke was a great cricket lover and admirer of Sir Donald Bradman, but unlike Menzies he did not have the sense of timing to 'do a Bradman' and retire voluntarily while still in front and not far down the other side from his peak.

It is a pity because some of Hawke's followers indeed had mapped out such a timetable for him. This provided for him to announce at the July 1991 centenary ALP National Conference that he planned to retire at the end of 1991, after a Commonwealth Heads of Government Meeting in Africa and a visit to Australia by US President George Bush Snr. If he had done that he would have cemented his position as a revered Labor folk hero and departed the political stage in a blaze of glory.

It was not to be. Instead there was a political assassination of him by a thousand cuts, which began with an extraordinary event of his own making. The series of developments which finally engulfed him went back to a fateful meeting at Kirribilli House on 25 November 1988, when he promised Keating he would hand over the leadership at a reasonable time after the 1990 election. In front of two official witnesses, businessman Sir Peter Abeles (Hawke's choice) and ACTU Secretary Bill Kelty (Keating's choice), this surely was one of the most extraordinary and mistaken secret political pacts ever made. Hawke was later to say: 'Against my basic judgement, but because I wanted to contain the relationship and maximise our chances at the 1990 election, I indicated that after winning the election I would, at some stage thereafter, step down as leader, clearing the way for Paul.'

When the 1990 election came and went and Hawke, basking in what he believed was a never-ending love affair with the people, showed no sign of moving—indeed he had promised the Australian electorate he would remain for another full term, so he could not keep both promises— Keating reacted.

'I am the Placido Domingo of Australian politics,' Keating told the 1990 annual dinner of the federal parliamentary Press Gallery, and what's more, he said,

'Australia had never had a truly great leader'. He did not mention Labor's Curtin, Chifley or Whitlam, and pointedly, he left out Hawke. The result: the aggravation between two mammoth egos surfaced publicly, news of the Kirribilli House deal was leaked to the media, and Hawke was seen to have reneged on his extraordinary promise to Keating. Then Keating mounted a first challenge to Hawke in June 1991 (and lost by 66 votes to 44) and began an unrelenting and long-range assault from the backbench. When the second Keating challenge came on 19 December 1991, Hawke lost in the Labor Caucus ballot by 56 votes to 51. This was a small but decisive margin. It was clear he had hung on just a little too long.

Partly because of this latter-day trauma in Hawke's period in office, it then became fashionable in some Labor circles in particular to criticise his record as a whole. This needs to be put in perspective. Before he went into Parliament in 1980 his career as ACTU president was marked by popularity, aggrandisement, aggression, achievement and personal controversy. He was a self-confessed womaniser and his behaviour under the influence of alcohol could be nasty. In particular a coarse performance in a public bar at an Adelaide Hotel after an ALP Conference where Hayden had bested him in a motion on prices-and-income accord policy has become the stuff of legendary tales.

After he left Parliament in 1991 his personal life, in which his marriage to his wife Hazel broke down and he married his biographer Blanche d'Alpuget, came brightly into the public spotlight. He patronised and savagely criticised Keating in his indulgent memoirs. He set out to use his extensive prime ministerial connections to make himself seriously rich as a businessman. Once hailed as the Messiah in the supermarkets of Australia, he found much of the immense public goodwill towards him dissipating.

All that is irrelevant in this context. Regardless of before or after, in his period in The Lodge, Hawke was a good Prime Minister and better than most. He was the ultimate competitor in everything he undertook: in golf, tennis, cricket, blackjack, negotiations and his main game of politics. He knew he had to give up drinking to get to the top and remain there, and he did. As he said in his memoirs: 'I addressed the question of drinking. I knew on the one hand I was not an alcoholic, but... I often behaved badly in drink.' He was a dreadful loser and hated to be seen losing, whether in a friendly cricket match between the press and politicians in Canberra or playing tennis against the Chinese Foreign Minister in Beijing.

Hawke strikes out in a golf game with Greg Norman at Royal Canberra in 1988.

He started his incumbency with two advantages. The first was that Hayden had prepared Labor for administration meticulously with a shadow ministry in which responsibilities were clearly designated and policies were well projected. Hawke inherited a true alternative government, ready to roll. The second advantage Hawke had was that, unlike Whitlam in 1972, he was not saddled with a Labor Caucus—the pool of MPs from which the ALP Ministers are selected—that had been languishing in Opposition for 23 years and clamoured for the spoils but not always the responsibilities of office.

Hawke had a new Labor generation of enthusiastic and generally pragmatic talent on which to draw. Button, Peter Walsh, Susan Ryan, Ralph Willis, Mick Young and Gareth Evans come to mind. And not forgetting Lionel Bowen, Hayden, Tom Uren and Keating, who had been Ministers in the Whitlam Government, though Keating had been one for only a few weeks. The result was stable government. Compared with previous post-Menzies administrations—those of Holt, Gorton, McMahon, Whitlam and Fraser—relatively few Ministers left in controversial circumstances, and Hayden, after six years as Foreign Minister, went to Yarralumla as Governor-General at his own request.

Unlike Malcolm Fraser, who insisted on a hands-on approach to every conceivable aspect of government, Hawke generally was happy to delegate administrative authority to his Ministers. He exerted his power-of-one on several notable occasions but he was a fine chairman of the Cabinet board.

For many years, until it turned horribly sour at the end, the Hawke-Keating relationship as Prime Minister and Treasurer was one of the most effective political combinations Australia has seen—rivalled later perhaps only by that of John Howard and Peter Costello.

Ever the extrovert, Hawke cultivated his Australian larrikinism with his constant 'G'day, mate', greeting to all he met. However, he found many parliamentary processes stultifying and was never really comfortable in Parliament itself. Indeed it was in the House that Keating demonstrated his superior prowess to their peers.

Hawke had made his view of Parliament dramatically clear seven years before he became Prime Minister. At a National Press Club address in June 1976, he floated the idea of having at least some ministers chosen from the community at large (as in the US system), instead of it being obligatory for them to be MPs (as in the Westminster system). The concept has merit. He said: 'What is peculiar about Parliament? The only thing that is peculiar about Parliament is that we inherited the bloody thing from that bloody little island 500 years ago. And I don't understand what's sacrosanct about that.'

Hawke never liked the confines of the Old Parliament House, and yet on the most historic occasion affecting it in his term, its closure as a Parliament in 1988, he rose to the occasion.

It was a night for nostalgia and celebration and after his final speech, all MPs and members of the Press Gallery sang 'Auld Lang Syne' and 'Waltzing Matilda' in the House. Hawke and John Howard, then Opposition Leader, linked arms to dance a jig, lead a conga in the main government corridor and together sang the Communist 'Internationale', hymn of the international working-class movement since 1871. Everybody there was surprised that both seemed to know the words.

Abroad, Hawke, albeit a small man physically who built himself up with high heels and puffed hair, walked tall on Australia's behalf. He was careful to make Papua New Guinea (followed by Indonesia) his first stopping-point on his first overseas trip as Prime Minister. It was both a symbolic and practical gesture, and the PNG Prime Minister, his genuine old 'mate' Michael Somare, warmly welcomed him. In colonial times, he had appeared for Somare in a landmark case aimed at improving the pay of PNG public servants.

On the other side of the world Hawke was idolised on a 1987 visit to Ireland, the first by an Australian Prime Minister, because of the deep Irish-Australia-ALP connection. At a ceremonial welcome in Dublin he made himself an honorary Irishman with a deft touch of blarney. He stood beside his Irish counterpart, Charles Haughey, and said he did not have a drop of Irish blood in him as far as he knew. But he was so pleased to be 'home'.

He was only the third foreign leader to address the Irish Parliament—the others being US presidents John Kennedy and Ronald Reagan. He spoke emotionally and with gusto. He made the point that the Irish form a greater proportion of the Australian population—one-third—than of the US population. 'Outside Ireland', he said, 'Australia is the most Irish of nations and we are proud of it.'

He said several Labor Prime Ministers of Australia, 'including the incomparable John Curtin and Joseph Benedict Chifley', had been of Irish extraction and that half his own Ministry claimed Irish origin. He rattled off names like Lionel Bowen, Paul Keating, Bill Hayden, John Kerin, Peter Walsh, Mick Young, Susan Ryan and Ros Kelly to 'satisfy even the most nationalistic among you'. The Irish MPs loved it. Charles Haughey announced a gift of a microfilm copy of 40 000 Irish convict records. Hawke was given a standing ovation.

After watching a strange football Test match between Australia and Ireland—played on a Sunday afternoon under a mix of Australian Rules and Gaelic Soccer and won by Ireland by 53 to 51—the one-time world beer-drinking champion decided to go on a pub-crawl to meet the locals. 'Mate, mate, this is terrific', he told all and sundry as he sipped non-alcoholic beer with some disdain. One bar where the Hawke crew turned up was closed. 'Sorry, it's the law on the Sabbath,' the publican said, 'would you like to come in and have one while were waiting for opening time.'

Later at Ryan's, reputedly the oldest pub in Ireland, dating back to the 16th century, Hawke, in casual open-necked drinking shirt, danced an Irish jig and sang 'Waltzing Matilda' and 'Danny Boy' with a traditional music group. Sticking to his non-alcoholic beer while all around him drank Guinness, he stayed to the small hours and reminisced wistfully how he had achieved the world beer-drinking record at Oxford in his student days—by downing a yard of ale, or 2.5 pints, in 12 seconds—and gone into the *Guinness Book of Records*.

Hawke also maintained a cordial relationship with the Republican administration in the USA headed by Reagan. This was thanks largely to a personal friendship with the US Secretary of State, George Shultz, who he had first met when he was ACTU president and Shultz was head of the Bechtel Corporation, a California-based international construction company. After Reagan's departure from the White House, Hawke maintained the connection with President George Bush Snr, and it was significant that he did not hesitate to commit Australia in support for the USA in the Gulf War.

Hawke's unquestioning affinity with Israel—where the RJ Hawke Memorial Forest had been planted in his honour during his ACTU days and now also stands tall—became balanced with a recognition of Arab rights, and he followed Whitlam and Fraser in opposing apartheid in South Africa and improving relations with China and Indonesia.

Hawke's greatest single achievement in foreign affairs, however, was his Asia-Pacific Economic Cooperation

(APEC) initiative, which he launched on a bitterly cold winter's day at the end of January 1989, in Seoul. He did so at a luncheon of Korean business groups in a particularly impressive performance, and one made more so by the fact that he had honed his thoughts and explained his concept to the accompanying Australian media party the night before, to make sure everybody got his message.

It was a visionary message, building on an earlier Hawke Government initiative which established the Cairns Group of Fair Trading Nations with the aim of breaking down the trade barriers imposed by the USA and the European Union. Hawke was a fine apostle. For the Australian correspondents, becoming understandably cynical about public relations overload and Hawke's normal penchant for hyperbole and convoluted sentences, his

Bob Hawke reveals his succinct command of the English language.

briefing that night in his hotel room in Seoul was masterful.

'I want to explain to you what I'm on about here, he began,' and he did, concisely and clearly. He answered questions, brought up new ones himself, batted ideas to and fro for the best part of two hours, and revealed he had raised the matter that day with South Korean President Roh Tae Woo. I realised this was how he had won many industrial negotiations in the past.

The outcome was all he had hoped for. Hawke strengthened his draft speech at the luncheon. Roh immediately brought South Korea on board. Momentum and favourable worldwide press coverage was assured. Foreign Affairs and Trade Department Secretary Richard Woolcott followed up with months of extensive work on the ground throughout the Asia-Pacific region. In November of 1989 came the first formal APEC meeting in Canberra, attended by Ministers from Australia, New Zealand, South Korea, the USA, Japan, Thailand, the Philippines, Singapore, Malaysia, and Indonesia. China, Taiwan and Hong Kong soon followed.

At home, the Hawke era saw much change in Australia. His government brought superannuation, held by only 39.5 per cent of Australian workers in 1985, to the masses. There were Budget surpluses until 1991 and a marked fall in inflation. His much-vaunted Accord with the unions improved industrial relations and there were fewer prolonged strikes—with, however, the notable exception of the pilots' strike when his Government brought in foreign and RAAF aircraft to break it.

Not since Chifley put troops into the coal mines in the late 1940s had military intervention been used in an industrial dispute. It was an event that marked the beginning of the end of the cosy two-airlines duopoly between Ansett and Australian Airlines

The floating of the dollar was taken against the advice

of Treasury Secretary hardman John Stone. Deregulation of the financial system, acceptance of foreign banks, privatisation of the Commonwealth Bank and Qantas came despite opposition within the Labor Party from those who adhered to the no-privatisation plank in the ALP platform. These were actions no Liberal-National government had ever been brave enough to take.

To his credit, one thing Hawke did not change markedly, however, was the public service. He slowed down its politicisation. He kept Sir Geoffrey Yeend, who had once been private secretary to Menzies, as Secretary of the Prime Minister's Department, and it was Yeend who advised Hawke on how Australia in effect could break completely from Britain, while retaining the Queen as sovereign, through the Australia Act of 1986.

Hawke also kept Stone on as Secretary to the Treasury when he took office, despite the reservations of many Labor Ministers at the retention of a man who they regarded as a Tory ideologue. In fact the abrasive Stone gave the Labor Government the same fearless and outspoken advice that he had given previous governments. Stone left the Treasury of his own volition, with considerable panache and with deliberate bad timing for the Hawke Government. Later, strangely and inconsistently, he joined the agrarian socialists of Bjelke-Petersen's National Party in Queensland.

On 15 August 1984, six days before Keating was due to deliver an annual Budget in the formulation of which he had been heavily involved, Stone arranged for a bottle of Veuve Cliquot and two glasses to be delivered to Keating's office, where the two were meeting. When the champagne arrived, Stone poured it out and handed Keating a glass and his resignation at the same time.

Hawke could combine emotion, which he never sought to hide, with pragmatism.

Ably assisted and abetted by Environment Ministers Barry Cohen and then Graham Richardson, he positively embraced the environment—significantly, with overall political success. As promised in the 1983 election campaign, he used Commonwealth powers to stop the Franklin Dam in Tasmania and set aside what became the Daintree World Heritage area in the wet tropics of North Queensland. More Tasmanian forests were protected. Uluru was handed back to its original Aboriginal owners and given World Heritage protection. Kakadu National Park was extended. The Great Barrier Reef Marine Park was enlarged to cover the entire reef.

He furthered the causes of multiculturalism, and of Aboriginals through the creation of the Council of Aboriginal Reconciliation. He danced in the sand with the Pitjantjatara people at Burunga near Alice Springs in 1988 and said he hoped there would be a proper and lasting reconciliation 'through a pact or treaty', however, he added a rider that he was not hung up about the precise word and what was important was the process. He raised expectations of Aboriginals over native title grants in Western Australia, but backed off when Labor Premier Brian Burke made his opposition clear.

Hawke's wishes prevailed, against a majority of Cabinet members, to stop mining at Coronation Hill. His voice trembled during his last official act as Prime Minister, in December 1991, when in Parliament House he formally accepted the Burunga Statement of reconciliation from the Aboriginal people.

Hawke cried openly for Israel, for a daughter with a drug problem, for his father the Rev Clem Hawke when he died, for China and the dead Chinese students of Tienanmen Square at a memorial service at Parliament House, Canberra.

His eyes watered, as did many others, at the most

moving event in my time with prime ministers, when he spoke at the Dawn Service and then Lone Pine, at Gallipoli in 1990 on the 75th anniversary of the Anzac landing, in front of an audience of remaining veterans of the campaign who had been flown over for the ceremony. It did not matter that we knew the actual words had been strung together splendidly by his speechwriter on that occasion, Graham Freudenberg, who had had an uncle who died at Gallipoli.

That Gallipoli visit also was marked by welcome bipartisanship on Hawke's part. He took along with him in his RAAF Boeing 707 the new Opposition Leader John Hewson and wife Carolyn. At the same time Veterans Affairs Minister Ben Humphreys flew to Gallipoli in the 747 jumbo chartered to carry the veterans, and took with him Tim Fischer, the National Party leader and Opposition shadow minister for Veterans Affairs. Fischer, a Vietnam War veteran and often a delightfully sincere eccentric, spent part of the afternoon of that April 25 swimming by himself in Anzac Cove, 'to get the feel of the water as it must have been'.

The Hawke era, however, was not without its turbulence, though he weathered most of the storms, generally with aplomb and apparent supreme confidence, credibility intact.

The first storm came in the form of the Combe-Ivanov Affair, in 1983, and Hawke solved that painfully, but as he believed, necessarily, by dumping on two Labor stalwarts: former party secretary David Combe, with whom he had worked well as ALP president, and special Minister of State Mick Young, hero of Gough Whitlam's 'It's Time' campaign in 1972.

In the case of Combe, then a lobbyist, the Hawke Cabinet suddenly declared Ministers were to grant him no access, after ASIO had convinced him Combe was associating closely with a Russian diplomat, Valeri Ivanov, who was a KGB agent.

In the case of Young, Hawke sacked him from his ministerial post after he revealed to close friend and journalist-turned-Labor-staffer-turned-lobbyist Eric Walsh that there was a Combe-Ivanov association and that Ivanov was about to be expelled.

In the furore that blew up in and outside Parliament, Hawke ordered a judicial inquiry into ASIO and the Combe-Ivanov affair. The Hope Royal Commission, at which there was the unusual spectacle of a Prime Minister taking the witness box and being cross-examined, subsequently vindicated Hawke's actions.

Young considered he had been badly treated and that Hawke—the 'silver bodgie' or 'Little Caesar' as he often referred to him—had over-reacted. Young never lost Labor Caucus backing and he later fought his way back into the Ministry. Combe, who was never found to have actually breached national security, eventually was supported by an ALP Conference and came in from the cold to embark on a successful career in private enterprise.

In retrospect the Combe-Ivanov affair was a reminder of the impact the Cold War had in Australia. It left nobody in any doubt on whose side was Bob Hawke. He was a Cold War warrior at ease with the Americans and relaxed about ASIO.

The Cold War was still alive and well in February of 1985, for instance, when along came the so-called MX-missile crisis—which Hawke solved quite easily by doing a blatant backflip. He had previously told the US Government (but not the Australian people) that US aircraft could use an RAAF airfield in Australia to monitor the testing of MX intercontinental missiles to be brought down in the Tasman Sea. This seemed innocuous because the Soviet Union also was testing missiles in the Pacific and Australia was in military alliance with the USA. But when news of the secret plan broke there was a serious domestic backlash, especially within the ALP and the trade union movement—and Hawke happened to be on his way to the USA, via Europe, at the time.

Hawke was in Brussels, where his main objective was to persuade the European Commission (EC) to lower its excessive levels of protection for agricultural products. But while he was lobbying away in the EC's headquarters, suddenly back home there were rebellious party calls for a special ALP National Conference to overthrow the MX arrangement. With his phone ringing constantly, Hawke quickly realised this. He also was alerted by Labor right-wing numbers men Graham Richardson and Robert Ray, who happened to be visiting Japan, about the depth of Labor feeling. Hawke decided overnight—in the Hilton Hotel in Brussels—to renege on the deal with the Reagan Administration.

He promptly asked his press secretary Geoff Walsh (later Consul-General to Hong Kong and at the turn of the century general secretary of the Labor Party) to tell the accompanying Australian media representatives at breakfast. This Walsh duly did and the reports sent immediately to Australia ended the anti-Hawke clamour within the Labor Party. But what would the US reaction be? This obvious question was put to Hawke that afternoon in the prime ministerial aircraft en route from Brussels to Washington. His confident response was that there would be no problem, that he had been in touch also with 'my friend George' (Shultz, US Secretary of State).

So it turned out. On our arrival in Washington a few hours later, the US State Department immediately assured us in rapidly revised briefing notes that there had been absolutely no harm done to the Australia-USA alliance. Shultz himself said mildly at a joint news conference with

Hawke that the USA had decided to conduct the MX tests without the use of Australian support arrangements.

As the ever-loyal Kim Beazley, then Defence Minister, was to say later of Hawke: 'Without doing any substantial damage to our standing in our relationship with the United States, he got George Shultz, against all the advice that George Shultz was receiving, to let us off the hook.'

The next pocket of turbulence came with the Tax Summit of 1985, when Hawke acted as an admirable chairman throughout most of the proceedings, and then intervened heavily. He let Keating have many days in the sun as Treasurer, zealously expounding the benefits of a proposed package that included a 12.5 per cent consumption tax. But when trade union opposition remained implacable, and ACTU President Simon Crean and Secretary Bill Kelty told him so in no uncertain terms at a late-night meeting in a Canberra hotel, Hawke killed it. The wheels suddenly came off Paul Keating's 'tax cart'. Keating never forgot.

There was one fiery blast of turbulence with which Hawke could do nothing but sit on the sidelines and hope: the trial of High Court Justice Lionel Murphy in 1986. Murphy was impeached for attempting to pervert the course of justice by asking a Sydney magistrate to help a 'little mate'—Sydney solicitor Morgan Ryan—who was charged with corruption.

In the upshot Murphy was found guilty in a first trial, but this verdict was overturned by the High Court. A second trial found him not guilty. The Opposition had a field day. Further allegations were being prepared when Murphy was diagnosed with cancer and died soon after. But for a while there we had a High Court judge, a former senior Labor politician and powerbroker, who technically at least, was a prisoner of the Supreme Court of New South Wales.

However, in yet another case of turbulence in which Hawke was a mere spectator, he could thank his lucky stars. This was the Bjelke-Petersen push for Prime Minister. It was at the Wagga Wagga (NSW) showgrounds, of all places, on a hot and dusty Saturday afternoon in January of 1987 that the Queensland Premier launched what turned out to be a bizarre campaign. He said he was about to oust Ian Sinclair as leader of the federal National Party, John Howard as leader of the federal Liberal Party, and Hawke as Prime Minister. Bjelke-Petersen declared he was lighting a 'bushfire' which would sweep across Australia. 'It's Wagga today,' he said, 'We'll make it Canberra tomorrow.'

The conflagration flared for weeks. John Stone helped give Bjelke-Petersen some credibility by apparently endorsing his flat-tax policy. Queensland National Party President Sir Robert Sparkes gave the campaign some organisational credibility.

The episode was weird. Bjelke-Petersen made overtures to South Australian Ian McLachlan—then the high-profile president of the National Farmers' Federation, which had a $10 million fighting fund—to join him. Bjelke-Petersen apparently believed he had McLachlan and the money lined up. The Joh-for-Canberra bushfire finally petered out when McLachlan rejected him. But not before Bjelke-Petersen had humiliated Sinclair, made further overtures to Andrew Peacock, broken the federal Liberal-National Coalition and burned and ridiculed Howard.

One of the most extraordinary and silly statements made by a political leader surely was that by Bjelke-Petersen, when he walked into a National Party Federal Conference at the Lakeside Hotel in Canberra, threw his hands in the air and exulted: 'Delegates, I have good news for you. The coalition with the Liberal Party is finished.' In the upshot Hawke, after initial hesitation, went to the polls early, in July of 1987.

Hawke made his notorious shorthand 'No child will be living in poverty by 1990' promise in his policy speech at the Sydney Opera House. He campaigned heavily on environmental issues. He capitalised heavily on his opponent's disunity. Labor's majority in the House of Representatives rose from 16 to 24. With good reason, Howard has never been in any doubt since that he would have won that 1987 election but for Sir Joh Bjelke-Petersen.

One of Hawke's most ambitious, worthy and even visionary domestic initiatives—an attempt to reform Commonwealth-States financial relations under his 'New Federalism' proposal—failed, thanks to Keating. Hawke floated the proposal at the National Press Club in Canberra in July 1990. In October of that year he formally launched it, with much optimism and with Keating sitting alongside as Treasurer, at a special Premiers' Conference in the old defunct Legislative Council chamber of the Queensland Parliament in Brisbane. Hawke's biggest ally was the only Liberal Premier, Nick Greiner of New South Wales, and all Premiers welcomed what they saw as a Commonwealth change of heart.

Following a subsequent Premiers' Conference, the proposal got as far as agreement that there should be a new revenue and tax-sharing scheme, and federal and State officials headed by Prime Minister's Department Secretary Mike Codd were working on the details. Yet it all came unstuck during Keating's leadership challenge. Keating, then on the backbench, in one dramatic speech to the National Press Club, completely sabotaged Hawke's 'New Federalism' concept, describing the surrendering of economic and other powers to the States as one of the gravest dangers facing Australia.

The States' high hopes that Hawke-type consensus

would lead to a solution of an antiquated financial system that impedes Australia's administration were dashed in the Keating era of confrontation. Queensland Premier Wayne Goss blamed the 'murky chemistry' of Canberra and deputy Premier and former ALP National President Tom Burns accused Keating of disloyalty to the Labor Party. In the angry aftermath, the Premiers, led by Labor's John Bannon of South Australia, went ahead without the Federal Government and formed the Council of Australian Governments—which is a nice-sounding and largely ineffectual body in which the Commonwealth, having joined up later, now inevitably is the core government anyway.

The Burns-Keating antagonism went back to 1969 when Keating first sought pre-selection for his Sydney seat of Blaxland and Burns, as party president, investigated allegations of branch-stacking and indeed found that Keating and his supporters had been so engaged.

However, just as there was no stopping Keating then, there was no stopping him 22 years later. Hawke was slow to respond to the challenge laid down by John Hewson's radically innovative 'Fightback!' package, and just as Hawke had done with Hayden in 1983, Keating, with Labor's NSW Right behind him, moved a second time. When the Labor Caucus gave its narrow five-votes-margin verdict against him, Hawke congratulated Keating and stepped down with dignity. The irony of the situation was not lost when he went out to Yarralumla to formally hand in his prime ministerial commission to Governor-General Hayden.

Hawke was given a standing ovation by MPs on all sides, not least from Hewson and the Liberals—and with Paul Keating noticeable for his absence—when he made his last speech to the House as Prime Minister. Resignation from his Melbourne seat of Wills followed early in the New Year.

By the time Hawke came to finishing his memoirs, his

Labor following had dropped away. Among the few Labor figures of the long Hawke era who attended the official launch of his book by Sir Ninian Stephen in August of 1994 were Michael Duffy (who had been Attorney-General), John Kerin (who had been Primary Industry Minister and Treasurer) and Bob Hogg (who had been ALP general secretary).

None of which worried Hawke, who went steadily on in his new career as a Sydney-based international businessman. He still was called in to solve the occasional industrial dispute as a consultant. After Labor's 2001 election loss, at the age of 73, the messiah of yesteryear became what the party hoped was a latter-day saviour, when he and Neville Wran were called in to recommend solutions to Labor's structural problems.

Keating

SYDNEY STREET-FIGHTER

Paul John Keating, Labor (1991–1996); 4 years, 2 months, 20 days.

'The United States has had three great leaders, Washington, Lincoln and Roosevelt. We've never had one such person, not one.'

Keating at the parliamentary Press Gallery annual dinner, 7 December 1990

'I have always thought that provided they [backflips] are done with the appropriate degree of panache and style, they serve a very useful purpose.'

Keating in 1992, after doing a reversal on television policy, comparing himself with US diver Greg Louganis, who won a gold medal for his backflips

As a youth Paul Keating occasionally sat at the feet of Jack Lang, the despotic Labor Premier of New South Wales who repudiated interest on overseas loans during the Great Depression. Lang's determination certainly rubbed off on the Sydney street-fighter from the wrong side of the tracks. Like Lang, Keating could be a great hater.

A self-made leader, lacking a structured education or formal qualifications, the eldest of four children in an Irish-Catholic family, he began his political apprenticeship walking the streets of Bankstown with his boilermaker father Matt, handing out union leaflets from a calico bag.

He arrived in Parliament in 1969, fresh from taking a local rock band, The Ramrods, to use his own words, from 'nowhere to obscurity'. He was imbued with the workers' cause after a stint as a clerk in the local council and a rise through the Labor Youth Council and he was slightly tarred with the brush of controversy over the branch stacking in his preselection.

Keating was 25. Six years later he became the youngest federal Labor minister in history when he was appointed Minister for Northern Australia, three weeks before the sacking of the Whitlam Government by Kerr. 'You're sacked, Keating', Whitlam snapped in the corridor of Old Parliament House on that portentous day, 11 November 1975. 'Why, what have I done?' Keating replied. 'We are all sacked,' said Whitlam, and strode on.

Fast forward to early 1983. When Bob Hawke rolled Bill Hayden neatly out of the Labor leadership with the help of the NSW Right-wing, Paul Keating—for once an out-numbered powerbroker in Labor's Right—was disconcerted. He believed the role of Labor leader after Hayden should have been his, and he was slow to join the Hawke bandwagon. But Keating put his ambitions on hold. With the popular Hawke installed as Prime Minister, he waited, yet with increasing impatience as the years rolled by. He was assuaged when Hawke agreed to an eventual handover at the extraordinary Kirribilli House meeting, but he bared all in his 'Placido Domingo' speech to the Press Gallery.

With that speech he also gave Hawke the opportunity to renege on the Kirribilli succession agreement. It was from that point that one of the best double acts in Australian political history, the Hawke-Keating combination at the top of the federal Labor government, quickly began to unravel.

In the young Paul Keating's tribal Labor world, there were mates and there were other mates. There were degrees of mateship. There was also deliberate antagonism. One of his favourite observations in times of Labor in-fighting was: 'I'm in the conflict business, mate, with a capital C. This doesn't worry me a bit.'

For Keating the ultimate mateship, the hardcore stuff, was in the club of the NSW Right. It followed that he was not a mate of Hawke, a Victorian. Nor at that stage, was he a mate of the ACTU's powerful secretary Bill Kelty, also a Victorian, or of Premier and ALP Federal President John Bannon, a South Australian (at the time credited with a 74 per cent popularity rating in public opinion polls).

Nor was he a mate of Queensland Premier Wayne Goss, or of Defence Minister Robert Ray, the Right's Victorian heavyweight, who he once described as the 'fat Indian', or Hayden, who had formed the Centre Left faction to counter the Right. It was Hayden who, shortly after being dumped as Labor leader, made that famous observation: 'Being called a mate by the NSW Right is like being presented with a bunch of flowers by the Mafia.'

Keating's oldest tribal mate was Laurie Brereton, who he met at the NSW Labor Youth Council in 1964. Brereton never failed to support Keating as he rose through the Labor organisation to become New South Wales president. Keating never failed to back Brereton as he rose to become a Labor Minister in New South Wales and then, after switching to federal Parliament, Industrial Relations Minister (instead of Simon Crean, former ACTU president and a Victorian) in the Hawke government. In retrospect it is ironic that after Keating had left politics, it was Brereton, as Labor's foreign policy shadow minister in the late 1990s, who became a principal critic of Keating's de facto endorsement of the 1975 Indonesian annexation of East Timor.

It was also ironic that when the Kirribilli House deal came about in 1988, Keating chose his old non-mate Bill Kelty, who had even persuaded Hawke to kill Keating's campaign as Treasurer for a consumption tax, to be his witness. Yet this was a reflection both of changing circumstances and Kelty's increasing respect for Keating's ability as a Treasurer.

For Keating had quickly developed from being a tyro in the job, dependent on Hawke in Cabinet and John Stone in the Treasury. He became dominant, knowledgeable and expert in his own right. He ran up a series of successive Budget surpluses. He implemented, with Hawke, the prices-and-incomes accord with the ACTU. He was named 'finance minister' of the year in 1984 by *Euromoney* magazine (which was roughly translated to the world's greatest Treasurer). And as he boasted, he kept his fingers on the economic levers and controlled the Reserve Bank. In May 1991, he became the longest-serving Labor Treasurer, passing Ben Chifley's 2996-day record.

Respect between Keating and Kelty became mutual and over the Keating-as-Treasurer years, Kelty became a key player in national administration, an outside mate with an inside running. Kelty became a member of the Reserve Bank board, a confidant of Keating in the big Hawke government decisions, from the floating of the dollar, to the deregulation of the financial system, to opening the economy to competition, to the sale of Australian Airlines, Qantas and the Commonwealth Bank, to implementation of capital gains tax, to across-the-board reductions in tariffs. The success of the Hawke-Keating duo owed a lot to Kelty.

Keating is in no doubt about who is in command.

The duo of course did not operate without tension, and most notably in 1986 when Hawke was on a trip to China and Japan. At home Keating decided to speak out about rising foreign debt and the need for the manufacturing sector to be competitive with the more technologically advanced industries in Asia. On John Laws' Sydney commercial radio programme he warned that if Australia did not get manufacturing going again and keep moderate wages outcomes and a sensible economic policy, it would end up being a third-rate economy. Keating said if growth slowed under 3 per cent, unemployment would rise again. 'Then you have gone,' Keating said, 'You know, you are a banana republic.'

In Beijing, Hawke's staff reacted more strongly than did Hawke and said Keating was trying to take control. Keating dubbed Hawke's minders the 'Manchu Court' and announced he was calling a special meeting of business, unions and the Government to discuss all aspects of the economy. Hawke promptly told the travelling media contingent in a background briefing there would be no such mini-summit as suggested by Keating and that he (Hawke) would make a 'state of the nation' address as soon as possible to assure Australia and the world that all was well with the economy.

When Keating finally crashed through into the prime ministership at that 56-51 Labor Caucus vote takeover in December 1991, he declared he felt very 'humble'. It was not a description normally applied, by friend or foe, to the Sydney street-fighter.

Yet this was a highly intelligent and highly articulate politician of great contrasts. On the one hand there was his public image. He was centralist, arrogant, dominant, assured, brutal and occasionally coarse in his use of invective. He was savage in his denigration of opponents. After John Howard became Opposition Leader (again) in 1995, Keating told Parliament: 'What we have got is a dead carcass, swinging in the breeze, but nobody will cut it down to replace him.' Howard, who in earlier days when they were both on the backbench had been on reasonably friendly, if detached, terms with him, had difficulty, even in private, of speaking civilly to him or of him when Keating was Prime Minister.

John Hewson, as Opposition Leader, was even more antagonistic and bitter. Hewson kept a painting of Keating on his office wall in Parliament House. Among other things, it depicted Keating standing on the heads of babies. This often startled visitors to Hewson's office and said something about the lack of professionalism in Hewson's approach to the job of parliamentarian.

Keating, though he had then been in Parliament for 22 years, seemed to care little for parliamentary proprieties, debate or processes. The House of Representatives was little more than a forum for him to demonstrate his authority. The Senate, in his mind, was composed of 'unrepresentative swill'. When asked if he would appear in any Senate committee inquiry into the controlling interest held by Canadian publisher Conrad Black in the Fairfax newspapers, he replied: 'I know my place in the world. I don't slum it before Senate committees.'

Like Whitlam, he underestimated the importance of the Senate, which is modelled on that of the USA and is possibly the most powerful Upper Chamber of any true democracy in the world. This was also the man who when asked how he determined if the Fairfax papers were balanced in their election coverage, replied: 'Well, I am the Prime Minister. That is how I become the judge.'

On the other hand was Keating's private persona. It is fascinating that speechwriter-historian Don Watson, in his *Recollections of a Bleeding Heart: A Portrait of Paul Keating PM*, should write of Keating's private introspection, uncertainty and melancholy.

Unlike the Rhodes Scholar Hawke, whose enthusiasm for cards, gambling, racehorses and all forms of sport was legendary, the little formally educated Keating had a passion for music, old clocks and art. When he was Treasurer and renting a house in Canberra, a common Saturday morning sight in the well-heeled suburban village of Manuka used to be Paul Keating in Abel's music shop, often by himself, occasionally with one or two of his children, earphones clamped to his head for an hour or two. This was the street-fighter at peace with himself, in a world of his own listening to Tchaikovsky or Beethoven or Rachmaninov.

With his wife Annita, a Dutch-born international flight attendant who he met on an Alitalia flight to Bangkok, he headed a very close and private family. Indeed, so much so that his passion for family privacy spilt over into public fury at needling Opposition questions about items such as renovations to The Lodge, the sacking of staff and a proposed purchase of a Thai teak dining table.

You can take the boy out of Bankstown, but... Keating responds to criticism of his spending on rare bird prints and a teak table.

This was the man who bought rare bird prints for the Cabinet room and when questioned on the cost said: 'You can't write a cheque for taste.' This was also the man who, when he diverted briefly from his duties as politician and Treasurer to relax, gave a lecture at the National Art Gallery in Canberra on

18th century French architecture, and amazed the cognoscenti in the audience with his knowledge and love of the subject.

From the outset as Prime Minister, Keating set out to make up for lost time and to apply his own agenda. He projected himself as the big-picture man, painting visions of black-white reconciliation, of a republican Australia enmeshing in Asia.

It surely was the Irish in him which partly motivated his drive for a republic, that and his gut political desire to go one step further than his predecessor, and the need to have distinctive issues of his own. His declared aim had long been to generate a 'touch of excitement'.

But first Keating had to stem the apparent Coalition tide. Hewson's 'Fightback!' economic and tax reform wave had surged forward in the public opinion polls in the wake of Keating's 'recession we had to have', and caught Hawke and Labor off-guard. Keating retaliated with a full-frontal attack on Hewson's proposed 15 per cent GST which ignored his own previous predilection for a consumption tax. He also threw in the republic issue, albeit rather mildly.

It was at Bankstown during his campaign speech for the election of 13 March 1993 that he proposed that a broadly-based group of eminent Australians prepare a discussion paper for a 'Federal Republic of Australia'.

The economic backdrop to the election did not favour Labor. Unemployment stood at 10.9 per cent of the workforce (down slightly from a peak of 11.3 per cent in late 1992) and more than one million people were out of work. Interest rates had been as high as 17 per cent on home loans and 21 per cent on business loans. Keating's once-high reputation as an economic manager had slumped.

Election night was poignant with expectation. Hewson waited at the Inter-Continental Hotel in Sydney, ready to celebrate, with business leaders and other supporters, for the

Coalition victory that never came. Keating waited at the downmarket Bankstown Sports Club. Against all the odds, Keating triumphed, and at Bankstown made one of the great off-the-cuff political speeches: 'This is the sweetest victory of all. This is the sweetest. This is a victory for the true believers, the people who in difficult times have kept the faith'.

Keating was confident he had a mandate in his own right to change Australia in the manner he believed best. Like Whitlam had been in 1972, he was the euphoric champion of all he surveyed. But Keating's mistake, in his hubris, was to believe he had won the 'unwinnable election'. In reality it had been Hewson who had lost the unloseable election because of his tax proposals and his inability to sell them properly.

Paul Keating both attracted and dispensed hyperbole. Many things said about him, good and bad, were exaggerated. Likewise much of what he said. He could combine private calm and public fury, sophistication and ruthlessness. If there was any single driving factor in his modus operandi, it was passion.

When he visited the village of Kokoda, at the northern end of the famous wartime track in Papua New Guinea, he was overcome with emotion and kissed the ground at the base of a memorial to the World War II Diggers. He was criticised by some opponents for carrying on like the Pope, which did not concern him in the least. When Papua New Guinea schoolchildren waved little Australian flags at him at a welcoming ceremony, he told one of them: 'Don't worry sonny, we'll get a new one of these soon.'

Sometimes his passion clouded his judgement. When he went to Villers-Bretonneux in France he was consumed with sudden anger at French intransigence in international trade and blasted his startled hosts—in a town in which the local people, remarkably, have dedicated to the memory of

Australians killed there in World War I. In this case his judgement clearly was astray, his sense of timing awry. I am convinced Keating's actions at Kokoda and Villers-Bretonneux were genuine and spontaneous.

This was a politician who learnt how to work the Press Gallery carefully and persuasively, yet when criticised by journalists was prone to making long phone calls of personal abuse to them. During one such diatribe, over an article of mine he disliked and disputed on details of his travel allowance, I decided I had had enough and hung up on him. He never phoned me again, with either background information or abuse. Needless to say, I was taken off the well-known government 'information drip'.

This was a man who could turn on his often-hapless opponents with lazy denigrating terms such as 'scumbags' and 'sleazebags', but who could also reveal touches of rare and telling humour. There was no better example of the politics of laughter at its best when, after Andrew Peacock became Liberal leader for the second time, Keating cooed: 'Can a souffle rise twice?'

Domestically, Keating is remembered as Prime Minister not so much for his sweeping economic policy (for that had been put in place basically when he was Treasurer) but for policies with a heavy, and for him, heady, overlay of symbolism... on a republic, on women in Parliament, on Aboriginal reconciliation, on the ceremonial interment of an Unknown Soldier at the War Memorial in Canberra.

Thus for Keating, as he said in an interview to mark 25 years in Parliament: 'The republic issue is not about changing the flag or insulting the Queen. It goes to the heart of our maturity as a nation.' Keating's classic expansion of this theme came in Parliament soon after Hewson attacked him for showing lack of 'respect' when he put his hand on the Queen's back to guide her through a throng at a reception in the Great Hall of Parliament House.

Goaded by this and by a British tabloid description of him as the Lizard of Oz, Keating lashed out: 'I was told I did not learn respect at school. I learned one thing. I learned about self-respect and self-regard for Australia, not about some cultural cringe to a country which decided not to defend the Malayan peninsula, not to worry about Singapore [in World War II]. This was the country [Britain] that you wedded yourself to and even as it walked out on you and joined the Common Market, you were still looking for your MBEs and your knighthoods and all the rest of the regalia that comes with it. You would take Australia right back down the time tunnel to the cultural cringe where you have always come from...'.

To put Keating's sweeping condemnation of Britain's wartime commitment to Malaya and Singapore in context, it needs to be noted he had an uncle who was captured at the Fall of Singapore by the Japanese in 1942 and who died on one of the dreadful Sandakan/Ranau death marches in 1945.

It is history now of course that Keating's desire to see Australia a republic by the start of the 21st century did not eventuate. But it was not for lack of trying. He appointed a Governor-General, former High Court judge Sir William Deane, who, under favourable republican circumstances, might have become Australia's first president. Keating also took his campaign as far as calmly and deliberately telling the Queen (of Australia) and the Duke of Edinburgh about his motives and plans, at a dinner at Balmoral Castle.

In contrast to his views on a republic, his attitudes to women were essentially conservative. In his maiden speech to Parliament in March 1970 he maintained the place for women was in the home as wives. This contention reflected the socially conservative Roman Catholic society in which he had grown up. He was highly critical of the Gorton

Government's boast that it had increased the number of women in the workforce. This, said Keating then, was not 'something to be proud of. I feel this is something of which we should be ashamed.'

Yet 24 years later, Keating was happy to accept the plaudits of the party faithful at the ALP National Conference in Hobart which unanimously endorsed an innovative quota plan to give Labor women 35 per cent of winnable federal and State seats by 2002. There were bouquets, hugs and kisses for him on stage at the convention hall at Wrest Point Casino as he did a jig with Carmen Lawrence and other women, and he declared: 'This will reshape the character of Australian politics and reshape the Labor Party.'

Keating's support for Aboriginal causes also became whole-hearted. When the High Court handed down its landmark Mabo decision in June 1992 which quashed the notion of 'terra nullius', the colonial proposition that Australia was unoccupied when settled by Europeans, he said: 'We now have the potential to do something real.' At Sydney's Redfern Park six months later, in a speech to mark the launch of the International Year for the World's Indigenous People, Keating said: 'The starting-point might be to recognise that the problem starts with us non-Aboriginal Australians. It begins, I think, with that of recognition. Recognition that it was we who did the dispossessing.'

Despite significant opposition—from the Liberal-National Party Coalition led by Hewson, from the mining lobby led by the Western Mining Corporation's Hugh Morgan, from many landowners, and from considerable sections of the general Australian community—and despite doubters and critics in the Labor Party, Keating was determined to give legislative effect to the High Court's Mabo ruling on native land title. In December of 1993, four days before Christmas, his Government's Mabo legislation finally passed in the Senate.

It was a negotiating triumph for Keating. The whole episode provided a classic example of his single-mindedness. It also contributed to his defeat in the 1996 election. But it made a difference. Aboriginals and whites had worked together in a grinding process in an attempt to find a practical solution to the land title problem. This was Keating painting the canvas of one of his beloved big pictures and then filling in the details.

Aboriginal leader Noel Pearson, who played a major role as a negotiator in the process, was to say later: 'Whitlam did the vision thing [on the indigenous land title cause]. Hawke did the crying thing. Keating did the doing thing.'

When he was in the mood, as he sometimes was, Keating could make great speeches. He could capture the moment. One of the finest speeches ever made by an Australian leader was crafted by Don Watson. Keating added the polish and the tone and he delivered it at the War Memorial on Remembrance Day, 11 November 1993. It was at the service for the Unknown Soldier, killed and buried on the Western Front in Europe in World War I, and finally brought home...

'We do not know this Australian's name,' Keating said, 'and we never will. We do not know his rank or his battalion. We do not know where he was born, or precisely how or when he died. We do not know where in Australia he made his home or when he left it for the battlefields of Europe. We do not know his age or circumstances—whether he was from the city or the bush; what occupation he left to become a soldier; what religion; if he was married or single. We do not know who loved him or whom he loved. If he had children we do not know who they are. His family is lost to us as he was lost to them. We will never know who this Australian was.'

'Yet he has always been among those we have honoured. We know that he was one of the 45 000 Australians who died on the Western Front. One of the 416 000 Australians who volunteered for service in the First World War. One of the 324 000 Australians who served overseas in that war, and one of the 60 000 Australians who died on foreign soil. One of the 100 000 Australians who have died in wars this century.'

'He is all of them. And he is one of us.' Keating had caught perfectly the atmosphere of Australia at war.

Overseas also, Keating was all for big-picture strategies, and especially in relation to Asia. He was ably assisted by Foreign Minister Gareth Evans, whose UN-backed Cambodia peace plan remains a positive legacy. Though he had killed Hawke's ambitious domestic 'New Federalism' concept, Keating fondly embraced, and quickly moved to enhance, Hawke's APEC initiative as foreign policy.

Keating expanded the scope and membership of APEC. He followed in Hawke's footsteps as one of the leaders of the APEC push. He was recognised as such by President Clinton at successful APEC conferences in Seattle and Osaka, and, in what were then happier days in Australia-Indonesia relations, by President Suharto at Bogor.

Yet even then his way with words could be risky. As when asked about Malaysian Prime Minister Mahathir Mohammad's refusal to attend the APEC conference in Seattle (mainly because of doubts about US motives), Keating replied: 'I couldn't care less, frankly, whether he comes or not... APEC is bigger than all of us, Australia, the USA and Malaysia and Dr Mahathir and any other recalcitrants.' It was a knee-jerk reaction which set Australia's relations with the prickly Mahathir back a long way.

With hindsight it can be seen that the Keating

Government's relationship with the Suharto administration of Indonesia, and especially his open admiration of Suharto himself, was too heady and unquestioning. The recent economic collapse in Indonesia, the East Timor independence agonies, and the post-Suharto political turmoil across much of the Indonesian archipelago are reminders of how short-term some relationships can be, particularly as conditions and governments change.

It is salutary to recall that at the time, on his first visit to Jakarta, Keating hailed Suharto as one of the world's great leaders and 'the region's undisputed elder statesman'. Keating said Suharto's military regime was a 25-year stabilising force for good in Australia's strategic area. The two established significant personal rapport. The Bogor Declaration of 1994 was praised as presenting an historic commitment to free trade in the Asia-Pacific by developed countries by 2010. Australia's relationship with Indonesia was likened in importance by Keating to the military alliance with the USA and the economic alliance with Japan.

Also in retrospect, possibly the strangest thing Keating did in this context was to negotiate a security treaty with Indonesia for eighteen months in secret. He first suggested it to Suharto at Bogor in June 1994. He used a former Chief of the Defence Forces, General Peter Gration, as his principal emissary, and the treaty came to fruition in December 1995 with a formal signing in Jakarta. It never became clear how binding it was, what it was meant to achieve, or exactly under what circumstances its provisions would be activated. Keating extolled it as the stuff of history, as did a few journalists caught up in the adrenalin rush. But many Australians did not like it being foisted upon them without warning.

In the volatile relationship Australia always has had with Indonesia, the treaty now appears not to have been worth the paper it was printed on. Yet it may have been handy to have had the official Australia-Indonesia amity of the Keating-Suharto years as the refugee/boat people pressures mounted in 2001.

Just as interesting was Keating's approach to Japan, with whom he subtly redefined Australia's relationship. In September 1992, during an Asian tour, Keating made it clear that Australia under his leadership would look to Japan in particular for friends and direction and guidelines rather than to the USA. He chose a ride in the Bullet Train from Tokyo to Nagoya, where he was to confer with the chiefs of the Toyota Motor Corporation on tariff levels, to give media representatives some background on what might have become an historic strategic policy shift by Australia. This was not the Keating who the previous April had kissed the ground at Kokoda in memory of Australian soldiers who died fighting the Japanese in World War II. This was Keating with another large and different picture to paint.

It was not, he explained, simply a matter of pragmatically keeping onside with Australia's biggest trading partner. Nor was it specifically a matter of Australia having to take the Japanese giant entirely on trust. Nor was it simply recognition of the clout exercised by the Japanese multinational car manufacturers, Toyota and Mitsubishi.

Nor, he said, was Australia walking away from the USA, with whom it had traditional ties and the long-standing military alliance of the ANZUS pact. Rather it was a reflection of his view that the economies of Australia and Japan were interlinked, that Japan's economic interests were Australia's interests, and that the more the economies could be interlocked the better. He twice said publicly in Japan that under his Labor Government, Australia would take part in no international pact or agreement that might harm Japan's interests. This was a comprehensive commitment. It also was typical Keating.

Came the 1996 election and the writing was on the wall. Keating was opposed by John Howard, who was much more politically astute than John Hewson and who had replaced Hewson's hapless immediate successor, Alexander Downer, in a well-managed bloodless coup.

In public, Keating maintained his flair and personal panache to the end. But he was dogged by allegations about conflict of interest because of a half-share investment in a piggery. He was also hounded by the resignation of Environment and Sports Minister Ros Kelly over a 'whiteboard sports-rorts affair', after her woeful inability to answer allegations of bias in her disbursement of community grants to marginal Labor seats.

Keating was plagued by his reputation for arrogance; by his disinclination to communicate with mainstream Australia the way Hawke had done, 'tripping over television cables in supermarkets' (Keating's words); by Bill Kelty's declaration of war 'with the full symphony' if the Coalition wanted a fight with the unions; and in particular by the 'It's time' factor. Labor had been in office for 13 years, its longest period since Federation.

Paul Keating himself laid much of the blame on the media, which he felt had starved him of the necessary oxygen of favourable publicity. He was particularly critical of the Canberra Press Gallery which he had once cultivated so assiduously. At his final National Press Club appearance before the election his mood was essentially that of a Prime Minister preparing for defeat, of a leader outlining his achievements for the history books.

Defeat, when it came, was substantial. The Liberal-National Party Coalition won 94 seats in the 148-seat House of Representatives. The Labor Party had 49 seats, a loss of 31. There were five Independents. Labor was reduced to a south-east triangle of seats, with 39 of its 49 seats being in New South Wales, Victoria and the Australian Capital Territory. Keating conceded quickly on election night and congratulated Howard.

It had been an anti-Keating election, but he was also defiant still: 'In the end,' he said, 'it's the big picture which changes nations, and whatever our opponents say, Australia has changed inexorably for the better.'

He was a better Treasurer than Prime Minister, but there was no doubt there had been his 'touch of excitement'. That was one objective which nobody would dispute he achieved.

He had known virtually no other occupation but politics. He was 52 when he left to undertake ventures in real estate and the financial markets and to give the occasional pungent lecture at the University of New South Wales. In the Howard era that followed there was, unsurprisingly, no role for him as a former prime minister. He would have hated it anyway. More's the pity.

Howard

MISTER ORDINARY

**John Winston Howard, Liberal (1996–?)
6 years, plus.**

'Would I ever seek the Liberal leadership again? No,
that would be like Lazarus on a triple by-pass.'
*John Howard after failing to beat John Hewson
in the wake of the 1993 election*

'A goods and services tax is not on our agenda, never
ever.'

Howard in 1995

John Howard arrived in federal politics in an era of Senate obstruction. He came to federal Parliament in the double dissolution election that Gough Whitlam called in May 1974, the election that hapless Liberal leader Billy Snedden said he had not lost, he merely had not won enough seats.

Howard, an ambitious lawyer from Sydney's lower middle class suburbs, would never have won party endorsement for the seat of Bennelong but for the unwavering patronage of Sir John Carrick. A former prisoner-of-war of the Japanese, Carrick rose to become the Liberal Party's general secretary in New South Wales, a Senator, a Minister, and government leader in the Senate. For two decades Carrick was the most powerful figure in the Liberal Party organisation in the nation's biggest city and most populous State.

Seldom have I witnessed such a whole-hearted endorsement of a political tyro as Carrick gave Howard at a 1974 campaign function in the now long-demolished Carlton-Rex Hotel in Sydney. 'This man, this candidate of ours,' said Carrick confidently (and he might well have added 'this lad of mine') 'will go right to the top.'

Twenty-two years later, Carrick's fearless prophecy, made in the face of doubters in the Liberal establishment, came true for Howard, after a rough roller-coaster ride. Mister Ordinary had achieved his ambition at last, with his most trusted and influential confidante, his wife, Janette, at his side. On the eve of the 1996 election he commented: 'If I'm not successful this time I won't be Opposition Leader and I won't be staying around.' He added, presciently: 'On the other hand, if I'm successful I'd see myself being in politics for quite a while.'

As Howard often liked to quietly and proudly boast at social gatherings, he was the first Liberal Prime Minister not to have been educated at a private school. His alma mater had been Canterbury High School, where he had failed at mathematics in the Leaving examination, but where he had shone as a debater.

When at the age of 56, he finally grasped the keys to The Lodge in Canberra—and to Kirribilli House in Sydney, which he and Janette decided to make their home—it was a fitting pinnacle for two political people who had met on Valentines Day, 1970—at a Liberal polling booth for a by-election where Labor's Laurie Brereton was making his run for the New South Wales State seat of Randwick.

Howard could look back on a few extraordinary highs and many lows. He had survived, and finally, against the odds and the forecasts, he had prospered. He was Treasurer in 1977. In Opposition in 1983, he was beaten by Andrew Peacock for the Liberal leadership, but became Opposition Leader in 1985. Battered by the Joh-for-PM campaign, he was beaten in the 1987 election and then deposed by Peacock. He was ignored by the Liberals when John Hewson became leader in 1990, and again in 1993, and again in 1994 when Alexander Downer was chosen by the party in tandem with Peter Costello to form a new generational 'dream team'. And eventually, he became leader once more, in 1995, by mutual consent with Downer.

Having failed to gain the leadership of his party on four occasions, he was at last on his way to becoming an entrenched Prime Minister after a bloodless coup! There has been no politician in this country more tenacious than the short, balding and bouncy John Howard. But he was never regarded as a 'messiah' in the manner of Menzies in the Liberal Party or Hawke in the Labor Party. Unlike Menzies he showed no signs of political humour. Unlike Hawke he carefully demonstrated little hubris.

The fact is that at the end of that roller-coaster ride Howard was just about the last Liberal of any standing left standing. Though he was certainly not a Constable Plod, he was a plodder. He was the tortoise who had won the race. In one moment of detached analysis, at a dinner for a few journalists I attended at The Lodge, John Howard admitted he had not won the 1996 election because the people regarded him as the greatest thing since sliced bread, but because most of them had come to dislike, even positively hate, Paul Keating.

For a long time, Howard was also the most inward-looking of Prime Ministers. If Keating in his aggrandisement was the self-styled 'Placido Domingo of Australian politics', in the mould of the visionary Franklin D Roosevelt, Howard in his deliberately humble self-projection, was the Harry S Truman.

Truman was reputed, when confronted with an issue and the need for a policy response, to have generally asked that homespun US rhetorical question: 'Will it play in Peoria?'—a reference to Peoria, Illinois, regarded as the core of the midwest heartland. In the same vein it could easily have been said of Howard that he constantly asked, as he went from issue to issue and policy to policy: 'And will it play in Ryde?'

Howard had several heroes, all white Anglo-Saxon, British-oriented to the bootheels: his grandfather and father, who had both served as Diggers on the Western Front in World War I, fighting for King and Empire; Winston Churchill (after whom he was named by his father, then a service-station owner, when he was born six weeks before the start of World War II); and Robert Menzies, Margaret Thatcher, and Sir Donald Bradman.

He appointed a pillar of the Anglo-Saxon establishment—the Anglican Archbishop of Brisbane, Peter Hollingworth—as Governor-General in 2001. Yet any such simplistic assessment of an uncomplicated man takes no account of the great Howard paradox: for this Mister Ordinary has been both a risk-taking economic reformist and a deep, introspective social conservative.

On the one hand, he promoted for years an ambitious agenda for financial, industrial relations, and taxation reform. Indeed he can be credited with contributing to setting such an agenda, even from the Opposition benches. As Treasurer in the Fraser Government he commissioned the Campbell report into financial deregulation, which was a bid to open up Australia's financial system in anticipation of the emerging economic globalisation he could see coming. He made virtually no headway against the die-hards, particularly of the National Party MPs, in the Coalition. Likewise, with John Hewson as his chief economic policy adviser, Howard was the first political leader to float the idea of a consumption tax, with the same net result at the hands of the Fraser Cabinet.

In Opposition, when Hawke and Keating opened the way for deregulation of financial markets, Howard repeatedly called for corresponding deregulation of the labour market. Howard was recognised as the leader of the Liberal Party's economic dries long before Hewson came to brief prominence with his 'Fightback!' manifesto as Liberal leader, though Hewson played a role in shaping Howard's economic philosophies in the first place.

On the other hand, well before he came to power as Prime Minister, Howard's track record as a social conservative was well and truly laid down, for all to see, in black and white.

There had been two great signposts in his first incarnation as Liberal leader. First, was his failed 'Future Directions' manifesto, when he went back to the 1950s with his ideal of a family with two children, a car and a house with a white picket fence, plus a dreadful campaign slogan tagged, with the help of Tony Eggleton (by then the Liberal Party's federal director), as 'Incentivation'. Second, was his thinly veiled criticism of Asian immigration in 1988, when he said, among other things: 'To me, multiculturalism suggests that we can't make up our minds who we are or what we believe in. I wouldn't want to see [the rate of Asian immigration] going any higher.'

Howard was backed solidly on this by National Party leader Ian Sinclair and John Stone, who was by then a National Party Senator, and the three of them were bitterly attacked by Ian McPhee, who as Immigration Minister in the Fraser Government had overseen the settlement of thousands of Vietnamese refugees. There were more small-l liberals in the Liberal Party in 1988 than there were in 2002. Howard ignored McPhee.

With a lot of political lessons learnt the hard way behind him, Howard finally came to office cleverly, with a broad-brush campaign based on motherhood statements and high aspirations, little policy detail and the voters' dislike of Keating. He promised there would be smaller government, fewer taxes on business, no GST, retention of Medicare and bulk-billing, a truly independent auditor-general, a statement of Budget honesty before each election, and a rebuilding of trust in politicians. He also promised an independent Westminster-type Speaker of the House of Representatives, a strict ministerial code of conduct, gun controls, retention of the Mabo Native Title Act (with the rider he would ensure it worked effectively), and a fixed percentage of revenue for the States.

He wrapped himself in the flag, stated his preference for the Monarchy, and remained philosophically attuned to traditions, conservatism, families, small business, mainstream middle Australia and a safe society. It was a sign of the times and of a despairing electorate that, during the campaign he was applauded most at meetings when he promised to rebuild public trust in politicians and Parliament. The Coalition did not win control of the Senate (no government had since Malcolm Fraser's in 1977) but it was back on the Treasury benches after 13 years of Labor rule. The times had finally suited Howard, as he had often (wrongly) forecast.

In office, John Howard's mettle was put to the sword early. As he was to do six-and-a-half years later in the wake of the Bali bombing, he rose to the occasion. On 28 April 1996, a deranged Martin Bryant, aged 29, gunned down and killed 35 people and injured 18 at Port Arthur in Tasmania. Howard seized the opportunity, read the wishes of most people in the emotional aftermath, and moved seriously to impose gun controls. He was the first political leader, federal or State, to do so.

This did not amount to a sudden anti-gun conversion by Howard. Quite the contrary. I remember a dinner I had with him in Canberra when he was well and truly in opposition after Hewson had defeated him for the Liberal leadership after the 1993 election. That night he seemed resigned to never becoming leader again. There had been a horrible neighbourhood shooting in Melbourne the day before. He said: 'I'm appalled at the shootings that go on in our suburbs and streets and homes. One of the things I would have liked to have done when I had some clout in office is to ensure there are fewer and less accessible guns in our community.'

In June 1995, after the improbable had happened and he was Liberal Leader and Opposition Leader again, he gave the inaugural lecture in the Menzies Research Centre's 1995 National Lecture Series. He described it as a 'headland' speech and said: 'Let me say that in the ebbing and flowing debate on the availability of weapons, I am firmly on the side of those who believe it would be a cardinal tragedy if

Australia did not learn the bitter lessons of the United States regarding guns... Whilst making proper allowance for legitimate sporting and recreational activities and the proper needs of our rural community, every effort should be made to limit the carrying of guns in Australia.'

When the tragedy of the Port Arthur massacre struck, Howard as Prime Minister did not hesitate. Though majority public opinion supported him (a Newspoll in June 1996 showed almost 70 per cent of the people thought that the new gun laws were appropriate), he received heavy flak from the rural heartland and gun enthusiasts. He showed considerable bravery politically and personally, to the point where his security guards told him to wear a body vest at one anti-controls rally he addressed.

He was backed fully on the guns issue by the new Opposition Leader Kim Beazley (who offered 'all strength to Howard's right arm') and by National Party leader and deputy Prime Minister Tim Fischer. There was opposition from the gun lobby and many National Party adherents in regional areas. Fischer was lambasted at one meeting as being 'a few wallabies short of a paddock'; a mistaken assessment if ever there was one. Howard finally forced through a comprehensive scheme in which many guns were bought back and many others were banned. It was the highest point in his first term as Prime Minister.

In other areas too, the Howard Government made a positive start. Howard seemed to mean what he had said about restoring trust in politicians. The promised Statement of Budget Honesty (requiring a government to reveal the latest budgetary figures at the beginning of every election campaign) eventuated. He announced a strict ministerial code of conduct. The new Speaker (Ron Halverson) was given due respect in the House. Treasurer Peter Costello quickly set out to bring the Budget back into surplus after Labor had taken it into the red.

But then, quite suddenly and sadly, both the reality and symbolism of trust and honesty was broken. The 'Honest John' image—derived, ironically, from a tag which Paul Keating had sarcastically given him in the 1980s when he was Treasurer—started to crack.

In the Menzies Lecture of 1995 Howard had said as Opposition Leader: 'I would rather promise half of what people might want and honour 100 per cent of it than commit myself to everything and deliver only half of it.' But by early 1997 as Prime Minister, he waved away many of his promises as non-core ones and unashamedly broke them.

A relaxed and comfortable Prime Minister defines his core and non-core promises.

His pledge to oversee a strict ministerial code of conduct came unstuck when it became clear he would not force several ministers—whose extensive shareholdings raised the question of conflict of interest—to observe the code. For example, John Moore as Industry Minister had a big industrial shares portfolio across the board and Senator Warwick Parer as Minerals and Energy Minister had a family trust holding mega-dollars in mining shares.

His promise to improve standards of parliamentary behaviour and to allow a Speaker to adopt a Westminster-type style came to nothing when Speaker Halverson virtually was forced out of the office—though Halverson's successors Ian Sinclair and Neil Andrew tried. Just as significantly, the outcome of Howard's 'never-ever' promise on a GST became one of the hallmarks of his administration.

Howard liked to refer to the 'broad liberal church' of the Liberal Party, capable of handling and enabling a congregation whose opinions and philosophies ranged across the spectrum. In fact he narrowed the Liberal Party's official focus. He oversaw one of the most radical reverse shifts in social philosophy since Federation. He never had been a small-l liberal and he now openly flew his colours as a big-L Liberal conservative. He became the undisputed Mayor of Middle Australia. He took Australia step by step further to the Right. Other parties in Parliament, with the exception of the Greens, followed.

It is interesting that what Howard liked to call 'mainstream Australia' appeared to accept this, mainly because for most 'middle' class people in suburbia the economy was running along pretty smoothly. There were protests from many interest groups as he continued to upset them—from what might be labelled generally as environmentalists, the public education sector, the public health sector, the social welfare lobby, small business, the human rights movement, feminists, ethnic groups, Aboriginals, the trade union movement. The list went on. Howard was unmoved.

There was important and often probing, though spasmodic criticism from his political opponents, and from columnists, including women and a few journalists, especially in the national Press Gallery. But this was partly counterbalanced by significant support from conservative and even racist radio talk-back hosts, especially in Sydney.

On the whole, the conservative Australian electorate did not get in a flap when the Howard Government cut funds for universities, for research, for social welfare, and for the ABC, all in the interests of economic rationalism and the budget bottom line. Nor was there much backlash when it disbanded the Commonwealth Employment Service and handed over many of the job replacement processes to the Catholic Church and the Salvation Army. Again, the electorate made little fuss when the Government used overriding Commonwealth powers to abrogate Northern Territory legislation which allowed voluntary euthanasia.

Voters did not erupt when their Government refused to ratify a United Nations treaty on the rights of women, when it voted against a UN motion condemning torture, when it was devious in its response to the challenges of global warming, when it reduced Radio Australia's penetration into South-East Asia, when it put boat people seeking refuge in isolated detention camps.

Despite considerable condemnation, he received a clear boost in public support, in August and September of 2001, when he refused to allow 427 asylum seekers who had been rescued from a sinking boat by the Norwegian freighter *Tampa* to land at Christmas Island for processing. Most people agreed with his stand that he was 'sending a message' to people smugglers in Asia and with his decision to stop more boat people with an expensive air and naval blockade. They also agreed with his ad hoc, novel and costly solution to transport these asylum seekers to the small islands of Manus and Nauru for processing—whence some eventually made their way to New Zealand and to Australia as accepted refugees anyway. People agreed that the Australian Government had to be able to run its own migration programme, whatever the merits or faults of that programme, in the face of the world's worst problems: terrorism, too many people and millions of refugees.

Most Australians also apparently agreed with his handling of what was loosely called the Pauline Hanson phenomenon—in which a former Liberal candidate overtly and covertly pushed the anti-Asian racist cause. Howard's response was first to ignore Hanson's simplistic One Nation push, then to equivocate, and finally to oppose it officially. At the same time, with Hanson no longer in Parliament but still running her campaign from outside it as she attempted to get back in, Howard's handling of the refugees issue started to bring One Nation sympathisers back to the Liberal fold.

There was no great furore when Howard raised politicisation of the public service to an art form by sacking several Labor-appointed departmental secretaries and putting department heads and other executives in the top echelons on short-term performance contracts. A few eyebrows were raised in Canberra, where people are closer to and more interested in the public service than elsewhere, and Menzies would have been appalled.

The valuable and traditional concept of ministerial responsibility was thrown overboard as senior public servants were made, on the whim of ministers, to take the rap for perceived shortcomings by their departments. The sacking of Paul Barratt as Defence Department Secretary in 1999 because the then Defence Minister, John Moore, did not like him, and the dismissal of Barratt's successor, Allan Hawke, in 2002 by Moore's successor, Senator Robert Hill, for the same reason, did nothing but harm for public service morale and objectivity. Where now the motivation for public servants to give 'frank and fearless advice'?.

But mainstream suburban Australia took little notice of these developments and the subtle consequences in public administration.

There was no great fuss when the Government abolished the Administrative Services Department and out-sourced much public administration and the handling of vast new information technologies to private firms and contractors in an ad hoc fashion which encouraged corruption. There was a little whistle-blowing from within the public service but no great public outcry when the Finance Department squandered a lot of money, millions of dollars, with its sales of public assets, including the Foreign Affairs Department's vast new complex in Canberra, and other government buildings which it then rented back.

On the ever-sensitive issue of reconciliation between indigenous and other Australians, perhaps the most indicative development was that it was the Governor-General of the time, not the Prime Minister, who took up the running and won acclaim from Aboriginals and their supporters. Sir William Deane was a practising Catholic and former High Court judge who had been in the affirmative in the Mabo judgement. As a Keating appointee, he was nicknamed 'Holy Billy' behind his back by some of Howard's ministers. He came ever so close to crossing the fine line which by convention separates the formal duties of a Vice-Regal figurehead from government policy.

But it was Deane who promoted reconciliation and other Aboriginal causes while Howard declared practical improvement of health and education facilities for Aboriginals was more important than land rights, described the High Court's Wik decision as a 'very disappointing judgement', and refused to say 'sorry' or take part in symbolic communal reconciliation marches. It was Deane who was applauded at a reconciliation conference in Melbourne and Howard upon whom Aboriginal delegates turned their backs.

All of which was like water off a duck's back to Howard, just as it was when the time came to play out the great symbolic issue of the 1990s: should Australia become a republic with its own head of state?

Whereas Paul Keating of Irish-Catholic background had deliberately promoted the concept of a republic by the turn of the century (and hoped Deane might be the first president), Howard of English-Protestant background and a convinced monarchist, effectively stopped the movement in its tracks, at least for some years. Howard did put a referendum question to the people, following a special convention in Old Parliament House, but then made clear his opposition to the question he put forward.

Without active prime ministerial support it was doomed to defeat from the start—because the referendum divided the pro-republicans into two camps, the minimalists and those who wanted to directly-elect a president—despite the fact that a majority of Australians were in favour of a republic of some sort. Howard hosted a special celebratory gathering of monarchists at Kirribilli House soon after the result was announced.

By the time the 1998 election came around it was clear that John Howard would live or die politically on the GST, the issue on which he had cast his lot. Having first advocated a consumption tax to no avail, then having staunchly backed John Hewson's 'Fightback!' attempt to introduce one, he said flatly, after Hewson's defeat in 1993, that as an issue it was dead. Five years later, the GST was the main plank of his 1998 election campaign.

One of the first hints that Howard was revisiting the

concept, despite his previous denials, came in a series of interviews he gave to various media outlets, including *The Courier-Mail*, in August and September 1996. He said: 'You know and I know the political realities. We were upfront in the Liberal Party about tax reform in 1993. We courageously advocated reform. We lost. The public said "no". And the Keating Government got another three years on the tail of that. We are now in government. We said [in the 1996 campaign] we weren't going to introduce a GST.'

But Howard continued: 'We have promised to conduct an in-depth examination of the tax system, so we have to look at the whole question of fiscal base-building. Let the debate go on about a GST. We made a commitment in relation to the term we are now in [in fact he said "never-ever", a mistake no politician should make] before the last election and that commitment stands. But that doesn't stop people talking about it and I don't want to discourage that.'

So the debate did go on, inside and outside the Howard Government. In 1999, after spending hundreds of millions of dollars of taxpayers' money on advertising, under the Government's name, on what was essentially a Liberal Party election plank—though the Government contended it was merely explaining the intricacies of the proposed new tax system to the people—the election was held.

The GST was the main issue, and the result was a net gain of 18 seats by Labor under Kim Beazley. But the Liberal's campaigned more effectively in marginal seats and there was a majority still of 13 seats to the Coalition in the House of Representatives. In terms of a two-party preferred vote, Labor did better than the Coalition, by 51 per cent to 49 per cent. Howard, mistakenly in my view, claimed a clear mandate from the people to introduce his revived GST, though it had not been his nemesis the way it had been for Hewson only five years earlier.

And so it came about, a hybrid complicated piece of tax law, by necessity watered down in both its impact and effectiveness at the request of the Australian Democrats whose support was required in the Senate.

In its first two years, it became clear that the Howard Government's GST was producing much revenue (which would benefit the States in particular), much paperwork for business, much anger among small business people, considerable difficulty in implementation by the Tax Office, and much confusion within the Labor Party over how to react. By 2001, however, the aggravation was subsiding and the Government could claim its tax and revenue projections were on track. The GST was overshadowed as a significant issue in the 2001 election by border controls and refugees.

It was in the wake of the 1998 election, however, that John Howard, he of the serious self-effacing image, became arrogant. As with all political leaders in office, especially those with a few substantial victories behind them, the hubris associated with the power of the post he occupied finally got to him. A sure sign and a symptom came when he declared that he as Prime Minister would stand in for the head of state, the Queen, and officially open the 2000 Olympic Games in Sydney.

At one private dinner at The Lodge with him, also attended by television commentator Paul Lyneham and Peter Cole-Adams of *The Canberra Times*, I asked him several times why he, as a declared monarchist, was insisting on what to me was a breach of protocol and tradition. He eventually replied: 'Because the Prime Minister is the most important and most powerful person in the country.' I came away from that dinner thinking for the first time that Howard, like his predecessors, had succumbed to the ego-tripping temptations which the office of Prime Minister provided. As it turned out, he was put off his Games-opening stride by public reaction which, as measured in opinion polls, turned heavily against him on this issue. He asked Governor-General Deane to open them instead.

When it came to foreign policy, Howard was often uncomfortable and cautious—until 11 September 2001. For several years he took little interest in Asia and less in the small Pacific Island nations where it was Australia's duty to take a lead. It was no secret that he did not hit it off well with the Democrat US President Bill Clinton. He was much happier with the relationship, and his government was much more accommodating to the US viewpoint—economic, military and environmental—after Republican George W Bush took over the presidency in questionable circumstances.

In one of his biggest foreign policy tests, Australia's roller-coaster relationship with Indonesia, Howard's approach to East Timor—favouring self-determination and independence—may have proved to be the harbinger of wiser long-term policy than that of Whitlam, Fraser, Hawke and Keating. The change in the relationship certainly had been rapid.

For it was only in 1995 that Labor's Foreign Minister Gareth Evans had written, in a book on Australia's Foreign Relations in the world of the 1990s, that since the Indonesian military annexation of East Timor in 1975, 'Australian governments, conscious of international realities, have accepted its irreversibility, with de jure recognition being given in February 1979' (by the Fraser Government). In the same publication, Evans praised Indonesia for its economic and financial reforms and confidently forecast: 'It is clear that by the turn of the century Indonesia will be both a massive and wealthy market.'

To the contrary. It is now history that Indonesia's economy collapsed, and that the Suharto regime was found to be corrupt and was ousted. It is also history that international pressure led to a UN-supervised ballot in which East Timor opted for independence, that the Indonesian military and militia forces then engaged in wholesale killing, and that a UN force led by Australia restored a semblance of order to one of the most battered little countries on Earth. And it is history that the Australia-Indonesia security treaty hailed by Keating and Evans with such enthusiasm suddenly was in tatters.

In 2001, few analysts disagreed with the assertion by Howard himself, albeit after his unnecessary Australian triumphalism and jingoism over the East Timor engagement, that his stand on East Timor had been pragmatic. If history proves anything, it proves that making predictions and wish lists, especially about foreign relations, is a risky undertaking.

When the horror of 11 September 2001—the terrorist attack on New York and Washington—hit, Howard was neither cautious nor uncomfortable. In Washington as it all happened, he immediately gave full support to the USA as Bush put it on a war footing. Rather quaintly, Howard soon after invoked the ANZUS treaty (in which the wording specifies allied action applies to the 'Pacific' area) with considerable flourish.

Howard had seized the advantage of incumbency in a time of crisis. Public support for him mounted. What had been seen by his critics as a miserable response to a mounting refugee problem became, in the minds of a majority of people, an understandable firm response to a problem of border controls and national sovereignty.

Throughout his extended political career, John Howard was tagged—by journalists, by commentators, by his official opponents, and by some of his own supporters—with two main attributes: first, he had staying power and was never to be underestimated as a politician; and second, he was narrow in his outlook as a leader, with a 'meanness of spirit'. Cartoonists and other satirists revelled in projecting him as a small Donald Duck type of suburban grocer, constantly counting the dollars and cents, or more aptly the pounds and the pennies in his 1950s till.

John Howard is stuck with the suburban grocer image...

However, he was a local storekeeper who knew what was going on in his street, and he did not bother to mince words about his likes and dislikes. For example he never really tried to hide his disenchantment with Bronwyn Bishop, who had made a reputation for herself as a steely-eyed inquisitor of public servants in Senate committee hearings. When she was starting to make a play for the Liberal leadership against John Hewson, John Howard told me, quite confidently, over dinner: 'She will get nowhere that matters.'

Howard could do nothing about the irreverence shown the nation's leader by the Australian press—thankfully, given the genuine nature of Australia's robust democracy. Thankfully also and to his credit, he would occasionally admit privately that he knew this. He once told me: 'This is not Zimbabwe, or Nigeria, or Yugoslavia, or Iraq, or Iran, or Pakistan, or China, or a host of other places I could mention.' And probably no Prime Minister worked the media, especially talk-back radio, more.

Yet the image of meanness persisted, as institutions from charities to universities felt the pinch, as queues for public hospital beds increased, as reports of appalling conditions in some nursing homes continued, as conditions for Aboriginals remained depressed, and as funding for many worthwhile non-government organisations was withdrawn.

The perception grew that just about everybody but those at the big end of town were worse off. Corruption, company failures and bankruptcies increased. The sudden collapse of Ansett Airlines, though largely the fault of its parent company Air New Zealand and the NZ Government, added to the economic worries and to the image of a Howard Government which could do little more than engage in ad hoc response.

Howard could not escape this projection, despite the fact that the Australian economy was doing better than most among OECD countries, despite extensive and expensive public relations exercises, and despite the fact that when his dry philosophy made him look increasingly wizened he projected himself as 'wet'. He made quite blatant policy backflips, for example on petrol excise, as he declared straight-faced he was 'listening' to the people.

For the mood of middle Australia was starting to change again. Many people now wanted better health and education facilities and better utilities, and some were even ready to forego tax cuts. Unrestrained economic rationalisation and globalisation, despite the benefits, were not perceived by all as the ultimate in economic and social progress. Some people, especially in the bush, would even have brought back 'Black Jack' McEwen if they could.

And then came 11 September, with all its known and unknown military, human, economic, international and domestic consequences.

John Howard, indefatigable campaigner, was right to be worried by the 'It's Time' factor as the 2001 general election loomed closer. But he was still what he had always been—underestimated and tenacious—and after months of trailing in the opinion polls he was in front again. As the Parliament was prorogued for the campaign, Beazley opined from the Opposition benches that Howard was the most considerable conservative politician Australia had produced.

It is recent history now that this assessment of Howard

was vindicated, and that Beazley himself, and his 'me-too' Labor Party, were rebuffed by the voters. The Liberal Party gained four seats (up to 68), the National Party lost two seats (down to 14) and the Labor Party lost two seats (down to 65).

As 2002 and a third term in office began, Howard and his wife had never looked more relaxed and comfortable. Nor had they looked more settled in.

Despite apparent increasing public concern from small-l liberals, the Howard Government maintained its hardline approach to refugees in detention centres. It came under serious fire in Senate investigatory committees in particular for its lack of compassion, and was trenchantly criticised by church leaders, by Malcolm Fraser, and by Neville Roach, former head of the Council for Multicultural Affairs, who resigned in protest against the Government's attitude. But their appeared to be no chinks in the Government's armour, no change in its thinking.

Phillip Ruddock might once have been a genuine liberal who in 1988 (at the time of Howard's comments on Asian immigration) crossed the floor of the House to vote with fellow Liberal 'wets' Ian McPhee, Steele Hall and Peter Baume to vote with the Hawke Government on a motion to return to a bipartisan immigration policy. But in 2002, Ruddock was still revelling in his mysterious transformation to Howard's impervious hardman as Immigration Minister.

At the same time any criticism from the UN was greeted by the Government with condemnation of the UN and its processes, and a majority of Australians still agreed. The weirdest foreign policy decision by the Government was to vote against a UN protocol which opposed torture of prisoners and detainees. In a line-up of nations, Australia sided with China, Libya, Cuba and the Sudan, against the EC and other democratic countries, with the USA abstaining. Most Australians took no notice.

At home, Howard had reason to be content with his lot. As the incumbent, for example, he could revel in making an upbeat announcement about a record export deal in natural gas to China. The new Labor leader, Simon Crean, in contrast, had to make do with announcements about reforms to his party's structure. Crean apparently could make no headway against Howard in the opinion polls and the Australian Democrats changed leaders and were in disarray.

The happy mildly-resurgent Greens—who had benefited in the 2001 federal election with support over policy on refugees from disenchanted Labor voters, in the 2002 Tasmanian election with support over forests policy from disenchanted Liberal voters, and in the October 2002 Cunningham federal by-election with support from disenchanted Labor voters—were kidding themselves if they thought they were about to form a powerful national third force.

When John Howard turned 63 on 26 July 2002, he was just twelve months away from the deadline he had set himself for when he would think about his future as Prime Minister. Nobody was more interested in what his thoughts might be than Peter Costello. In an uncertain world and region—suddenly made more so in October 2002 by the Bali bomb outrage—most Liberal MPs were coming to the conclusion that Howard would say: 'Not yet'.

Epilogue

Over the past half-century the political pendulum has swung back and forth. In 2002, Labor was in control of every government in this over-governed country except the Federal Government. It held the reins in all six State governments and the two Territory governments. According to the opinion polls, the Labor Premiers of South Australia and Queensland were the most popular politicians in Australia.

But Labor did not run the overriding Commonwealth Government that really matters—the one with the purse strings.

Who can tell what the state of play will be at the end of the 21st century's first decade? The only certainty is that the wheel of fortune in politics always and eventually turns, even in dictatorships. This is the fascination of it all. Sooner or later the wheel will turn in Australia, one of only seven countries which went through the entire 20th century as a genuine parliamentary democracy. The others are Britain, Canada, New Zealand, Sweden, Switzerland and the USA.

After observing the political and parliamentary scene for a reasonable period from the superb vantage point of Canberra, I have several laments.

The first lament is that parliamentary standards have seriously declined, and public distrust in MPs has risen accordingly. The House of Representatives has not been a proper debating chamber for many years, or a place for elucidation of many facts or ideas. It has become little more than a cockpit for theatrical combat for the benefit of 30-second grabs on television.

This debasement of the House by the Executive has become progressively worse as each government has gone and the next one has come. The Senate, where no party has an absolute majority, is a better forum, and parliamentary committees are much better at delving into the myriad concealed mysteries of public administration.

My second lament, alluded to throughout this book, is that just as the House has become increasingly sidelined as the nation's most important forum, so the public service has become more and more politicised. It apparently will take a very resolute Prime Minister to reverse this Americanisation of Australia's administration, because this would require virtually a change of culture.

My third lament is that humour, serious Australian funniness, true sophisticated mickey-taking, has disappeared from politics. I quote a few examples from the past:

Angry woman repeatedly criticising Menzies at an election rally: 'I wouldn't vote for you if you were the Archangel Gabriel.' Menzies: 'Madam, if I were the Archangel Gabriel, you wouldn't be in my constituency.'

Interjector repeatedly interrupting Whitlam as he outlined Labor policy during an election campaign: 'Yes, but what's your policy on abortion.' Whitlam, eventually: 'In your case, I wish it was retrospective.'

Whitlam to Clyde Cameron at a Labor Party executive meeting discussing economics: 'What would a f—-ing ex-shearer know about economics?' Cameron: 'As much as a classical Greek scholar.'

Senator Justin O'Byrne to a Tasmanian senator who asked why the Commonwealth could not pay costs in maternity cases: 'You mean assisted passage?'

*

Let me give some examples of clever and sophisticated parliamentary parry-and-thrust in which there is no need for 'scumbag' language:

On how to hit hard, yet with polite maturity, where it really hurts: Eddie Ward to Menzies (who had a commission in the citizen forces before World War I, but at the request of his parents, who already had two other sons at the war, did not join the Australian Imperial Force): 'The Right Honourable gentleman had a brilliant military career, cut short by war.'

On how to pour scorn on an opponent: Menzies to Calwell, in the lead up to the 1963 election: 'It is essential that they [the USA] know whether the Australian people stand behind our clear-cut statement, or prefer the ambiguous, fluctuating and almost mumbling attitude of our opponents.'

On how to reply to such an attack: Calwell to Menzies: 'You throw off at my voice. I can't help it. It is the voice that God and nature gave me. Unlike the honourable gentleman's, it is an Australian voice. It is not a mixture of Oxford, affectation and adenoids.'

On how to deliver a fine and simple eulogy: Whitlam, on the death of his political opponent, Sir Wilfrid Kent Hughes, an MP of great propriety: 'If he so often walked alone, he walked a very straight path.'

On how to disagree with the Speaker and get away with it: Clyde Cameron to Sir William Aston, in 1970: 'This is the thing that amazes me, sir. I know how sage and wise you are on most occasions, but here we have this inexplicable lapse on your part—a lapse I cannot account for because you are not a silly person. You do not look stupid.'

On how a Speaker can combine humour with authority: Speaker Archie Cameron, to a Labor MP whom he called to order for shouting and who replied he had never shouted: 'That is right. Your friends have told me about that.'

On how to couch a personal attack in reasonable language: Paul Keating on Opposition Leader John Hewson: 'I was implying that the honourable member for Wentworth was like a lizard on a rock—alive, but looking dead.'

On how to be a serious practical joker: As when 'Black Jack' McEwen received a note, apparently from Liberal backbencher Dudley Erwin, which read: 'Next time I ask you a question, McEwen, don't try any of that Smart Alec bullshit answer you gave the House this afternoon.'

At the same time, Erwin received a note, apparently from McEwen, which read: 'Congratulations on your splendid question this afternoon. It gave me the opportunity I had been waiting for to explain that situation. Could you kindly come to my office at 3 o'clock for a cup of tea. Fond regards, Jack.'

A delighted Erwin promptly called at McEwen's office for his cup of tea and friendly discussion. But when Erwin's arrival was announced by a secretary, a furious McEwen stormed out, shouting: 'Don't you ever send me another note like that, you infantile bastard! My answer was not bullshit. It was a statement of fact.' Erwin was shattered.

When they both eventually settled down and showed each other their respective notes, they realised they had been hoaxed. They blamed Killen.

*

Of course, not all the quotable quotes from the past have been deliberately funny, though some have been hilarious. For example: Kep Enderby, a Minister in the Whitlam Government, once observed with a wise manner: 'Historically, most of our imports come from overseas'; and Senator Reg Wright as Works Minister: 'Murder carries the penalty of execution by death.'

My fourth lament is aimed at some media commentators and MPs who use the word 'Canberra' as shorthand for the 'Federal Government' and/or its bureaucrats. As in: 'Thanks to Canberra, the GST tax bungle is getting worse,' or 'If Canberra could only come to its senses, we would not have this mess in education and health.'

My point is that Canberra, the national capital, is a city of more than 300 000 people, mostly ordinary multicultural Australian citizens. It happens to be the seat of government and so also has a diplomatic corps, a defence headquarters, a public service, and lobbyists.

Cabinet generally meets there to make its decisions. Parliament passes legislation there. Of the 224 MPs (148 Members of the House of Representatives and 76 Senators), only four (two Members of the House of Representatives and two Senators) actually come from Canberra. The rest all come from somewhere else in Australia. They are not cocooned in an ivory tower.

My fifth lament concerns the grand building, the $1.1 billion construction on Capital Hill which is Parliament

House, and the adverse effect on its inmates. The decision to build it was taken by Malcolm Fraser's Government and he has since admitted that he may have made a mistake.

I have never liked it. I remember shocking Bob Hawke at the party in the Great Hall to commemorate its opening in 1988 when, as he was extolling its virtues, I said: 'Mussolini would have been proud of it.' Hawke's reaction: 'Mate, that is simply disgraceful.'

It is a splendid piece of architecture. It has fine artefacts, tapestries and portraits. It is a good place for public functions, with its Great Hall. It provides good facilities for its inhabitants, including committee rooms, a first-class library, dining room and swimming pool. It provides a splendid lesson in how to put thousands of cars (used by visitors from all over Australia and the 3000 people who work in the building) underground, instead of in ugly above-ground parking lots.

But, if the core definition holds that a Parliament is a House of and for the people, it is not a good Parliament building. It is too big. It is a clinical building. It is a remote building.

The distance around it is two kilometres. Ordinary members of the public who come there find it hard to relate to their MPs who are away behind locked doors in a secure area. MPs do not relate properly to other MPs. Senators do not relate properly to Members of the House of Representatives and vice versa. MPs find it hard to see Ministers, let alone the Prime Minister. Administration of the nation suffers as a result.

Unfortunately, too, some members of the Australian media, under tight time constraints and finding it harder to gain access to MPs and Ministers in the building's vastness, do not try as much as they should. Much information within the building comes by handout from spin doctors, by fax, email and phone, rather than by person-to-person contact.

At the same time, either media proprietors do not invest as much in resources in the Canberra Press Gallery as they should, or too many journalists coming into the Gallery regard a stint there as a stepping stone to somewhere else.

The most respected are the ones who are steeped in the place. Not enough are making the reporting of federal politics and government from a Canberra base their career. Yet as a base, Canberra is still the best place for a journalist who wants to be in on the serious action. The national Press Gallery is still a bastion of competitive journalism. The loose 'rat pack' tag is nonsense.

However, laments aside, it's been a pleasure.

Finally, for a little frolic and controversy, I have compiled my ideal cross-party Cabinet, a First Fifteen from the politicians I have known. There should be no more than 15, for I cannot understand why, when there are 17 public service departments (which easily could be reduced to 15), the system should require 30 or more Ministers and more than 10 parliamentary secretaries to administer them. This is jobs for the boys and girls gone mad. In Washington, the central administration of the federated United States of America has an executive president heading a Cabinet of 22. When Menzies took Australia into World War II in 1939, he had a ministry of 15.

My First Fifteen, comprising five Liberal, three National, and seven Labor MPs, is:

1. Prime Minister: Sir Robert Menzies (Liberal)
2. Deputy Prime Minister & Aboriginal Affairs: Bob Hawke (Labor)
3. Foreign Affairs: Gough Whitlam (Labor)
4. Trade: Sir John McEwen (National)
5. Treasurer: Paul Keating (Labor)

6. Attorney-General: Sir Garfield Barwick (Liberal)
7. Education: Malcolm Fraser (Liberal)
8. Health: Bill Hayden (Labor)
9. Defence: Kim Beazley (Labor)
10. Primary Industry & Regional Development: Doug Anthony (National)
11. Secondary Industry & Industrial Relations: John Button (Labor)
12. Environment: Barry Cohen (Labor)
13. Immigration: Harold Holt (Liberal)
14. Social Security: Dame Margaret Guilfoyle (Liberal)
15. Transport & Communications: Tim Fischer (National)

Since every government needs fiery, forensic and effective opposition, I would put these 15 people on the Opposition frontbench:
1. Opposition Leader: Eddie Ward (Labor) marking Menzies
2. Deputy Leader: Reg Withers (Liberal) marking Hawke
3. Shadow foreign affairs: Sir Paul Hasluck (Liberal) marking Whitlam
4. Shadow trade minister: Bert Kelly (Liberal) marking McEwen
5. Shadow treasurer: Peter Costello (Liberal) marking Keating
6. Shadow attorney-general: Lionel Murphy (Labor) marking Barwick
7. Shadow education minister: John Gorton (Liberal) opposite Fraser
8. Shadow health minister: Jenny Macklin (Labor) marking Hayden
9. Shadow defence minister: Sir James Killen marking Beazley
10. Shadow primary industry & regional development minister: John Kerin (Labor) marking Anthony
11. Shadow secondary industry & industrial relations minister: John Howard marking Button

12. Shadow environment minister: Graham Richardson (Labor) marking Cohen
13. Shadow immigration minister: Arthur Calwell marking Holt
14. Shadow social security minister: Fred Daly (Labor) marking Guilfoyle
15. Shadow transport & communications minister: Ian Sinclair (National) marking Fischer

What a lovely mix of mainly incompatibles! All these people would have to be in the House of Representatives. Party allegiances would be discarded. The Senate would be retained, with all its current immense powers as a genuine chamber of review, but with no Ministers in it.

To keep the House in order, I would have Sir Billy Snedden as Speaker. He has easily been the best. As Governor of the Reserve Bank I would have Ian MacFarlane, who is the first person in that position to really try to explain to the people what he is on about, and Michael Kirby would be Chief Justice of the High Court.

And riding shotgun, ready to act as vice-regal supremo as Governor-General (or nominal President as head of state) at Yarralumla when the constitutional or political need arose, would be Sir Zelman Cowen.

What fireworks! What fantasy! What fun!

ABOUT THE AUTHOR

Wallace Brown is a veteran political journalist. After working in London and New York for the *Herald and Weekly Times*, he has been in the National Parliamentary Press Gallery since 1961, representing *The Courier-Mail*, Brisbane, most recently as National Affairs Editor and commentator.

During his time in Canberra, he has covered 17 general elections, 38 annual Budgets, 10 Prime Ministers, 8 Governors-General, and 11 Opposition Leaders.

He is a foundation member and former President of the National Press Club, former Vice-President of the Press Gallery, a former member of the Old Parliament House Redevelopment Committee, and recipient of an OAM for services to journalism.

Index

INDEX

INDEX